# DIVORCING

# A PARENT

Also by Beverly Engel:

*The Right to Innocence*

# DIVORCING A PARENT

## FREE YOURSELF FROM THE PAST AND LIVE THE LIFE YOU'VE ALWAYS WANTED

BEVERLY ENGEL, M.F.C.C.

Fawcett Columbine • New York

This book is dedicated to my dear friends
Sharon, Joy, Patti, and Linda,
who have stood by me
through *my* divorce and
who have become my new family.

# ACKNOWLEDGEMENTS

I would like to express my gratitude to the following people who helped make this book possible:

- ☐ Janice Gallagher for her outstanding editing and invaluable input, for her encouragement and honesty, and for recognizing the importance of this book from the beginning.

- ☐ Ted Mason for connecting me with Janice and Lowell House.

- ☐ Patti McDermott for her excellent feedback and encouragement from the beginning of the project.

- ☐ Linda Riggs for her continual support, encouragement, and feedback.

- ☐ Joy Davidson, Ph.D. for reading the manuscript and giving me some excellent suggestions.

- ☐ Sharon Kwast for reading parts of the manuscript and for her input.

- ☐ Roxanne, Connie, and Marjorie for writing parts of their stories so that others might benefit from their experience.

- ☐ All my clients past and present for their openness, courage, determination, and constant inspiration.

- ☐ Don Olderberg from the *Washington Post* for interviewing me and writing an article on "Divorcing A Parent" and for inspiring me to write the book in the first place.

- ☐ Derek Gallagher for his patience, dedication, and hard work.

- ☐ Mary Nadler for her excellent copy editing.

- ☐ Lise Woods for her valuable marketing.

- ☐ Tanya Maiboroda for her tasteful jacket design.

- ☐ Patti Cohen for her assistance with publicity.

- ☐ And everyone from Lowell House who made working on this book a wonderful experience.

# CONTENTS

## AUTHOR'S NOTE

In this book, "parent" may represent either the singular or the plural, depending on your situation, as may "parents." I also alternate between using the pronouns "she" and "he."

# DIVORCING

## A PARENT

# My Own Decision to Divorce— and Yours

Many people do not understand why someone would want to "divorce" a parent. In fact, most people are critical of the very idea. Divorcing a parent is a sensitive and often controversial issue that until now has not been addressed formally, although anywhere from one-fourth to one-half of all adult children from dysfunctional families choose to divorce one or both parents.

I understand the guilt, anger, fear, and pain that those who contemplate this decision feel; the courage and commitment to healing and recovery it takes in order to make this decision; and the agony of mourning the loss of the parent. I am an expert on the subject of child abuse and for fifteen years have been a therapist specializing in working with adult children of dysfunctional families. I also understand personally the plight of the adult child who must make this monumental decision, because a few years ago I had to divorce my own mother.

Like most adult children who decide on divorce, I had tried for years to work things out with my mother. I entered therapy for the sole purpose of releasing my anger and resentment toward her because of her neglectful and abusive behavior toward me when I was a child.

1

Not all divorced parents are abusive monsters. In fact, they are often well-meaning people who do not intend to be as critical, controlling, or neglectful as they are. I believe that at times my mother had good intentions toward me. I know she worked hard to learn how to communicate with me. She even came into therapy with me a few times. She also admitted to being a selfish person, and for years she tried to be less so. She apologized for having neglected me during my childhood, and she seemed to have a real understanding of how that neglect had affected me during both my childhood and adulthood.

I didn't divorce my mother for what she did to me as a child, however; through therapy, I had been able to work through most of my anger toward her for her abusiveness. The reason I divorced her was that I finally came to the realization that I was risking both my emotional and physical health by being around her.

Even though I was an adult with a successful career, loving friends, and a good relationship, inside I was still a little girl trying to please my mother, hoping that I could somehow please her enough for her to love and accept me. In the few years before our divorce, our relationship had seemed to be improving. Several years earlier my mother had undergone cancer surgery, and that difficult time had brought us closer together. She seemed to have mellowed because of the surgery, and she acted more caring toward me. But as time passed, she reverted back to her old ways, becoming increasingly demanding and critical of me. No matter how much time I spent with her and no matter what I did for her, it was never enough.

Because I was getting emotionally healthier, I began to realize that my mother never asked about my career, my relationship, or for that matter, anything else about my life. I also became frustrated because she would not open up to me emotionally and tell me anything about herself, other than sharing mundane things. We spent most of our time together running her errands. We seldom had any good conversations, and we became increasingly uncomfortable with each other.

I slowly grew aware that after each time I visited my mother I felt diminished and negated. It began to take me longer and longer to recuperate from a weekend visit. After being in her presence for only a few hours, I would be extremely tired and depressed and would feel dizzy for days. Finally, I went to the doctor for a checkup and discovered that I was suffering from a stress-related condition. My doctor urged me to reduce the stress in my life in order to avoid more serious problems.

I immediately knew what stress I needed to eliminate. I started going to see my mother less and less, and when I did visit her I stayed for only a few hours instead of for the entire weekend. She became more and more unhappy with the situation, calling me up frequently to complain. There were always things she needed me to do, and she would try to make me feel guilty for not taking care of them for her. I tried to explain to her that I hadn't been feeling well, but she didn't even ask what was wrong. It hurt me to realize that she cared so little.

I soon noticed that the more time I spent away from her, the better I began to feel. I went to see her only out of guilt, for when I did visit her, I always suffered emotionally and physically. One of the last times I saw her, I was shocked when I realized that I could take out the bottle of medication that the doctor had prescribed for me and take a pill, and my mother would continue talking to me without missing a beat. She never asked what the medication was for. I was slowly coming to the painful conclusion that my mother did not love me, and never had.

I had determined a long time before that I was not going to let anything get in the way of my personal recovery, that I could let go of anything or anyone who got in the way of my growth. It was a tremendous step for me when I realized that I had to let go of my mother, the only family I had. It felt at once liberating and extremely frightening, but I did it—and I feel freer now than I have ever felt in my life.

The longer I have stayed away from my mother, the stronger I have become. My self-esteem is higher, I am less angry, and my relationships have improved greatly. Just recently, I saw a made-for-television movie called *I Know My First Name Is Steven*, about a boy who was kidnapped by a man who then molested him and held him captive for seven years. I became very upset by the movie, but I didn't understand why until I suddenly realized that I felt as though I had been held captive all my life by my mother. Like Steven, I wanted desperately to escape, but I had nowhere else to go. My mother made me feel that I was lucky she was willing to work to put food in my stomach. She would threaten me that if I didn't mind her, she would send me away to a convent.

Even after I'd left home, I still felt that my mother had control over me. It's hard to explain why, except that there was a part of me that was still afraid of her, of her wrath and disapproval. It wasn't until recently, after I hadn't seen my mother for two years, that I realized I no longer felt like her captive. It took divorcing her to finally make me feel free.

Although you may not know it, there are thousands of other people besides you who wish they didn't ever have to see or hear from their parents again. It isn't that they don't love their parents, but that they feel unsafe with them. Sometimes they feel physically unsafe because their parents are still physically or sexually abusive, but most often they feel *emotionally* unsafe because of verbally abusive, controlling, overly critical, or neglectful behavior that has been going on since they were children.

It is not my intention to tell you in this book that you should divorce a parent or that you shouldn't. You clearly need to decide this on your own. Instead, I would like to explore with you the positives and negatives of doing so and offer support for whatever you decide. With enough support and perspective, you can make a healthy choice.

No matter what you have endured in terms of abuse and neglect, you have the potential to live the rest of your life in a far healthier way than you have lived so far. You aren't condemned to putting up with a parent who is abusive, neglectful, or controlling. While you didn't have a choice as a child—you couldn't leave your parents' household, no matter how abusive they were to you—you do have a choice now. Divorcing a parent is indeed a radical choice, but it is a very viable one, considering what you have been through and continue to go through with your parent or parents.

*Divorcing a Parent* applauds those who have the courage to take such a drastic step—even when continually pressured by society, family, and friends to "forgive and forget"—seeing it as the significant, life-affirming decision that it can be.

You may decide that you want to divorce a parent and that you feel ready to do so now. Or, you may choose to try a "trial separation." Many adult children temporarily separate from their parents while going through the recovery process to see how it feels to be away from them and their influence. On the other hand, you may realize that you are not ready to divorce or temporarily separate or that you do not want to divorce your parent at all. Divorcing a parent is a very complex issue, and *Divorcing a Parent* provides you with alternatives: temporary separation, physical divorce, emotional divorce, or reconciliation. It equips you to make the right decision for yourself.

There are no absolutes. There is no right way to divorce a parent, no guaranteed way to cope with the loss and the pain, and no magical way to deal with the pressures and criticism of others. Having said that, I can still take you step by step through the decision-making process, prepare you for the final good-bye, help you through the grieving process, and help you learn how to deal with feelings of guilt and with pressure from others.

In the first part of the book I will help you to decide whether or not you wish to divorce your parent. Topics include good and bad reasons for divorce, when it's time to stop trying, and how to prepare yourself for the act. In the second part of the book I will talk about how to implement the divorce; what to expect in terms of your own and others' reactions; what to tell your children, and how to decide whether they should be allowed to continue a relationship with your parent; how to deal with holidays; how to cope with a illness or death of your divorced parent; how to divorce a parent after his death; and what to do if you should change your mind and want to reconcile.

No one should have to continue a relationship that is abusive, destructive, or unhealthy. Yet, many adult children continue such relationships with their parents. Since it is acceptable to get divorced from a spouse who is abusive or detrimental to our growth and well-being, why shouldn't it be acceptable to do the same with a parent? *Divorcing a Parent* offers hope to the many thousands of victims of childhood abuse who still suffer even as adults from the constant abusive behavior of their parents.

# PART one

# To Divorce or Not to Divorce

# CHAPTER 1

# Anatomy of a Divorce

"I wish there was some way I could divorce my mother." I can still clearly remember the first time I heard a client voice the words that I had been silently thinking to myself for years. Heather was recovering from extreme childhood physical and emotional abuse. A recovering alcoholic and an adult child of an alcoholic, she had been encouraged to forgive her mother by the teachings of her Alcoholics Anonymous groups.

"I know it was her alcoholism that caused her to be abusive, and I know I'm supposed to work on forgiveness, but I just can't seem to," she continued. "I think I've forgiven her, and then she tells me what a creep she thinks I am or what a disappointment I am to her, and all the old pain comes back. Even if I could forgive her for the past, I can't keep forgiving her for hurting me over and over now. There's got to be a time when forgiveness ceases and self-preservation takes over. How can I continue to recover if she continually undermines my self-esteem? I really wish I never had to see her again!"

Through the years, I have heard many clients say they wish they never had to deal with their parents again. Most of these clients were either physically, sexually, or emotionally abused as children; many, like Heather, are also adult children of alcoholics.

All came from dysfunctional families. Because of my own experience with my mother, I know how these clients feel. And unlike many therapists, I do not think the answer to our conflicts with our parents necessarily lies in trying to understand our parents better or in forgiving them. In fact, I do not believe that forgiveness is necessary or even possible in some cases. Instead, I began to suggest another option—that of divorcing a parent who continues to be abusive, controlling, or neglectful.

Until quite recently, the idea of divorcing a parent was not a popular one. Most therapists have encouraged their clients to have empathy for their parents and to learn to forgive them for their mistakes, no matter what the parents may have done. This focus on forgiveness and understanding has also been reflected in many popular psychology books. In the past, several excellent books have been written about resolving the conflicts between adult children and their parents. Most notable have been *Making Peace with Your Parents,* by Harold H. Bloomfield; *Cutting Loose: An Adult Guide to Coming to Terms with Your Parents,* by Howard Halpern; and *My Mother, My Self,* by Nancy Friday. These books have all been useful in helping adult children to understand their parents better and in teaching them more effective ways of communicating with their parents in order to help break negative patterns of relating. As my client Heather experienced, Twelve-Step recovery programs also teach the philosophy that we should forgive our parents because they were doing the best they could with what they had and because they, too, were damaged by their parents. In addition, most religions teach us to forgive others and to try to forget the hurts they have done to us.

## IT'S NOT SO EASY TO FORGIVE

But as wise as all these therapists, books, and philosophies are, forgiveness is difficult and sometimes impossible. In reality, there are thousands of people who, no matter how hard they have tried to understand their parents, cannot forgive them. In fact, for many adult children it is impossible to forgive or forget, since their parents committed such horrendous crimes against them. When a parent has locked you in the closet for hours, beaten you to the point at which your body is bruised or broken, burned you on the arms and legs with cigarettes, deliberately put your hands in the fire, or brutally raped you, it is difficult or impossible to forgive him or her. And it is equally difficult to forgive a parent who has committed a crime against someone else—beaten one of your siblings to death, battered your mother for years, killed someone in a car accident while drunk, or sexually abused your siblings or your own children.

Oftentimes the crimes parents commit are not as brutal as those listed above but are just as damaging and difficult to forgive. Perhaps your parent abandoned you when you were a child by literally deserting you, by giving you away to someone, or by leaving you with others for long periods of time (days, weeks, months, or even years). He or she may have left you alone when you were too young to take care of yourself, or left you to wait alone in a car or in your yard for hours at a time.

Perhaps your parent severely neglected you by not providing the nurturing, attention, and protection you needed. Neglect can include withholding adequate nutrition, clothing, or shelter; refusing to obtain treatment for an illness or impairment; not providing adequate supervision or hygiene; disregarding health hazards in the home; or not allowing a child to attend school.

When Kathryn was growing up, her mother would leave her and her sister alone outside for the entire day, bringing them into the house just before their father returned from work. They were usually given nothing to eat for the entire day and were only allowed to come inside the house to use the bathroom. If they cried and begged long enough at the back door, their mother would sometimes throw them something to eat, such as a raw potato. They saw no one, spoke to no one, and had no one else to be with except each other.

Kathryn's mother is obviously a very cruel woman, as evidenced by the way she so blatantly neglected her children. But even after her children grew up she continued to be cruel to them. Whenever Kathryn spoke with her on the telephone, her mother would berate her, hang up on her, call back, yell obscenities at her, and then hang up again. Kathryn went into deep depressions after such calls, and at times she even became suicidal. As hard as she tried not to, she took in some of her mother's accusations. Kathryn finally came to the conclusion that in order to save her own life, she would have to sever all ties with her mother.

You, too, may have thought what a relief it would be to never have to deal with your mother or father again. But this desire probably appalled and shamed you. Because of the focus on forgiveness within the religious, psychological, and self-help communities, adult children have not been given permission to have such feelings and have been made to feel wrong for having them. Many people view divorcing a parent as unforgiving and vindictive. But when you successfully divorce a parent, you are not doing it to get back at your parent or to punish him. Nor does divorcing a parent necessarily mean that you *haven't* forgiven him. Some parents continue to be so abusive, critical, or controlling that their adult children must divorce them in order to save themselves from further damage.

More and more therapists who specialize in working with adults who were abused as children are discovering that forgiveness is not necessary for healing, and that forgiving a parent is not necessarily the healthiest choice in all situations. Sometimes, forgiving a parent is like giving him or her permission to continue being abusive.

## YOUR NEEDS ARE IMPORTANT

Aside from the pervasive belief that we should forgive our parents, there are other reasons why it can be difficult for you to give yourself permission to even consider divorcing a parent. To divorce a parent is to make the strong statement that you are terminating the relationship as a way of taking care of yourself. In our society, we are often taught that it is selfish to think of ourselves and our own needs first; in addition, many people who decide to divorce a parent grew up believing that their needs were not important. If they took their needs to their parents, they were often ignored, rejected, or told that they were being too demanding or selfish. Because of this, they learned to hold back their needs in the same way that they learned to hold back their feelings. They were taught to take care of their parents' needs instead and, in some cases, to actually serve as "parents" to their parents. These children were often given such nonverbal messages as "I can't meet your needs—I have too many of my own," or "I didn't get my needs met when I was a child, so you have to take care of me now."

Further, most parents in dysfunctional families are not good role models for their children in how to properly attend to one's own needs. You may have watched helplessly while your mother was brutally beaten by your father, only to watch her take him back again and again. Or you may have listened while your alcoholic mother verbally berated your father, tearing him down in front of everyone in the family, only to hear him begging *her* for forgiveness later on. With these role models and with your early training in taking care of your parent's needs, it is no wonder that you may have felt that divorcing your parent would be out of the question. After all, you have been brainwashed into thinking that your own needs are unimportant and that taking care of yourself would be selfish.

Your needs—including the needs to be respected, valued, listened to, believed, and accepted for who you are—*are* important. And you have rights—the right to run your own life the way you want to, to make your own decisions and your own mistakes, and, ultimately, to break away from an abusive, critical, or controlling parent if he or she is interfering with your right to a happy, healthy life.

Because you were not taught to take care of yourself, you may not even know how to do it. Instead, you may automatically shift into the caretaker role, anticipating and meeting the needs of others, putting others' needs first and sacrificing your own needs. Even though you may desperately want to get away from your parent, you stay trapped by your need to be *understanding*. One client of mine, Linda, said to me, "How can I expect my mother to be understanding and accepting of me when I can't be understanding of *her*? She can't help the way she is—that's the way she was raised. I need to try to accept her the way she is—with all her faults, and not criticize or abandon her just because she isn't what I'd like her to be. If I did that, I'd be no more understanding then she is. If I want understanding and acceptance, I need to give it."

While these words sounded convincing, they were actually very saddening, since they were coming from a woman whose entire life had been damaged by an extremely critical, even sadistic mother. No matter what her mother did to her, no matter how often she was deeply hurt by her mother, Linda would turn the other cheek and try even harder to please a woman who refused to be pleased.

Linda had been raised to believe that taking care of herself or even thinking about herself were very selfish acts. When Linda was a child, her mother was constantly saying, "Stop thinking of yourself all the time! No, you *can't* go out and play—I work hard all day, and the least you can do is stay home and take care of your brother and clean this house." Consequently, Linda learned to sacrifice herself for the sake of others—most notably, her mother.

## DIVORCE IS DIVORCE

Another reason you may have had a difficult time giving yourself permission to consider divorcing a parent is that you feel that you must keep trying, that you must "put up with" your parents' behavior no matter how destructive it is. Many people feel trapped and hopeless because they don't know they *can* divorce a parent. But divorcing a parent is really not much different from divorcing a spouse. While there certainly are people who remain in marriages because they feel stuck, most people today do not stay in unhappy marriages for long. Most know that even though divorce is painful, staying in an intolerable situation day after day, month after month, is even more painful. And so, even though they are afraid of the loss and pain, they proceed with the divorce because they at least have the hope of a better life afterward. Generally speaking, even though feelings of failure may accompany a divorce, divorce is often seen as a healthy step.

The same concept holds true for any relationship. If we have a friend who betrays us or who is selfish, unreasonable, or critical, we do not usually keep this friend very long; if we do, it is because we are caught up in an unhealthy pattern. By the same token, if we have a boss or supervisor at work who is unreasonable, demanding, unfair, or abusive, we don't usually remain passive and allow this person to continue behaving this way toward us. If all our attempts to resolve the problem fail, the healthy thing to do is to quit the job, however reluctantly, because we refuse to be treated so poorly. This kind of action is seen as an assertive one, based on the ability to value ourselves and on the belief that we deserve better treatment.

When it comes to divorcing a parent, however, the rules somehow change. The decision to divorce a parent is usually not seen as a healthy one. People who decide they can no longer tolerate unfair or abusive treatment from their parents are frequently regarded as selfish children who think only of themselves and who are not magnanimous or patient enough to cope with a few difficulties.

"But blood is thicker than water," you may say. "My parents will always be in my life, and that's the way it should be." Does that mean that no matter what a person does to you, or how unhappy you are with him, you must continue the relationship because he is your parent? Why should we put up with behavior from a parent that we would never tolerate from a friend or a mate?

We have just as much right to divorce ourselves from a parent as from a spouse. It is exactly the same concept. Think about the reasons why people divorce. In most cases, it is because one or both parties are so unhappy with the relationship that they want out. They may have found that they cannot resolve the problems between them, or they may simply have discovered that they are so radically different that there is no way to get along. Perhaps one feels so hurt by the other that he or she feels unable to forgive and forget. If the spouse continues to be emotionally, verbally, physically, or sexually abusive, divorce becomes a question of survival. Or one partner may find that the other is an obstacle to their personal happiness and well-being. These are exactly the reasons why adult children sometimes divorce their parents.

It is important that you realize that all the reasons why married people divorce are just as viable when it comes to divorcing a parent. And it is even more important that you realize that the decision to divorce your parent may be the only available alternative when the relationship is so destructive that you must choose between your health—both emotional and physical—and your parent.

What exactly is divorcing a parent? According to *Webster's*, "to divorce" is "to terminate an existing relationship." As with any divorce, divorcing your parent is a declaration that you are no longer "bound" together, that you are no longer "responsible" for each other, and that you are severing all ties. It is also a declaration of the end of any attempt on your part to forge a close bond. In some cases, it means a cessation of all contact, while in others it means a reduction of the contact to important occasions such as weddings and funerals, or to special holiday greetings such as Christmas and birthday cards. Either way, as Howard Halpern, the author of *Cutting Loose: An Adult Guide to Coming to Terms with Your Parents*, writes, "It marks the end of any frequent, regular, or expected contact and an abandonment of further attempts to wrestle emotionally with your parents about the nature of the relationship."

Isn't there some other way that adult children can resolve their problems with their parent instead of going to the radical extreme of divorcing them, you might ask? Can't therapy or Twelve-Step programs help them to let go of the past or to learn healthier ways of communication? The answer to this question is both yes and no.

Yes, therapy and Twelve-Step programs can certainly help adult children let go of the past and learn healthier ways of relating to their parents. But adult children often find that they cannot do it alone. Just as in a troubled marriage, both people must be willing to work on the relationship in order for it to be mended. Unfortunately, many parents are so stubborn or so dysfunctional that they refuse to look at themselves and refuse to change. When this occurs, the burden falls on the adult child to somehow adjust to the way the parent is—a burden that is sometimes impossible to bear. Unable to accept the way their parent treats them, these adult children are forced to divorce themselves from their parent in order to insure their own health and recovery.

## LOOKING FOR REASONS IN ALL THE WRONG PLACES

It is important to be aware of some of the negative motivations for divorcing a parent, as these are guaranteed to cause you further pain. The purpose of divorcing your parent is to take care of yourself, to protect yourself from further damage and pain, and to help facilitate emotional separation. It is not to punish, blackmail, or try to control your parent. Stated simplistically, divorcing a parent should be something you do *for* yourself, not something you do *to* your parent.

Some of the following reasons given for divorcing a parent are positive and self-affirming, while some are negative and self-defeating. Which do you think are the positive ones?

1. "I'm tired of trying to make my mother see how she ruined my life. She just gets defensive and refuses to listen. I'm so angry with her I could scream. In fact, the last time I talked to her on the phone, that's exactly what I did! I decided then and there that I would divorce her. Maybe then she'll miss me and be sorry for what she's done to me."

2. "I have to divorce myself from my father for my very survival. I can't stand any more of his deliberate undermining of my recovery. I've tried everything, from joint therapy to family meetings, but he simply refuses to listen or to even consider changing."

3. "It has taken me a long time to finally admit to myself that my parents are bent on destroying me. They try to rob me of any self-esteem, they've destroyed my relationship with my wife, and they've turned my children against me."

4. "I decided that the best punishment for my father for what he did to me was to just stop seeing him. I know he misses me, and that makes me feel vindicated somehow. He wasn't there for me when I was a kid, and now he knows what it's like to feel alone."

Paragraphs two and three are positive reasons for divorcing a parent, because they are based on taking care of oneself and saving oneself from the destructiveness of a parent. Paragraphs one and four, on the other hand, are negative reasons, because they are based on getting revenge or on "teaching the parent a lesson." In the following sections we will discuss in depth some of the wrong reasons for divorcing a parent and how you can make sure you don't fall into these traps.

### "I'll Show You!"

When you began to realize that one or both of your parents were abusive to you and that you were still suffering from the effects of that abuse, you probably became very angry with them, and rightly so. You may have decided that instead of working on releasing your anger in constructive ways, you would punish your parent by ignoring him or her. You may have convinced yourself that your parent was not worth any effort on your part, and that releasing your anger was just a waste of time. But to divorce a parent when you are still enraged is a very unhealthy thing to do. If you release the majority of your anger first, then you can be sure later on that your motivation is not to punish your parent but to take care of yourself. Divorcing a parent out of anger may tie you to him or her even more than before.

We all know married couples who decide to divorce because they are angry with each other or because one or both is bent on revenge. While divorce is supposed to be a final action, in some cases we see that it is used only as a weapon to hurt the other or as a battleground for further arguments. Some couples going through divorce engage with each other constantly, albeit negatively, and so there is no "break" in the relationship at all. They remain tied together through their constant battling.

With the help of a professional therapist, you can find constructive ways of releasing your anger so that your decision to divorce will be based not on anger but on your need to do the healthiest thing for you. Until you have released a great deal of your anger you may continue to stay cut off from your other feelings toward your parent, such as hurt and love. If, for example, you do not know that you also feel hurt by your parent, you may not know that you also have love for her. Your anger may keep you stuck in hating her. No matter how abusive your parent was or still is, because she is your parent you will probably always love her. This is true of every adult child, and it is completely normal.

Divorcing a parent needs to be done with the full recognition that even though you love your parent, you need to let go *for your own good.* Therapy can help you to get in touch with all of your feelings toward your parent and to build your self-esteem so that you will have the courage to do what is best for you, whatever it is.

## "You Either Change, or Else!": Emotional Blackmail

Divorcing a parent needs to be a healthy choice, not a neurotic one based on manipulation and attempts to control. Furthermore, if your decision to divorce your parent is an attempt on your part to change him, to force him to finally see the error of his ways, you are not divorcing him at all—you are still attached to and invested in him. Here are some questions to ask yourself to help determine whether you are still trying to change or control your parent(s):

Do you try to tell them how to run their lives?

Are you excessively critical of them, pointing out their faults whenever you have contact?

Do you frequently argue with them?

Are you echoing your parents' abusive behavior by being abusive to them?

Do you constantly rehash with them what they have done to damage you, belaboring the same issues?

Do you continue to blame your parents for all your current problems?

Do you believe that the only way you are going to feel better is for your parent to change?

The more you try to control, the more out of control you will feel—and the more out of control you feel, the stronger will be your desire to control. Attempting to control your parent will only leave you increasingly frustrated and confused.

The only real control worth fighting for is that over your own destiny. When you were a child, you did not have control over your life. Your life was dictated by what your parents and other caretakers wanted, not by what you wanted. Now that you are an adult, no matter how much your parents may try to control you, they can't unless you allow them to. But neither can you control them. They will have to learn their own lessons and make their own changes voluntarily. Trying to push them into changing will only make them defensive and keep you neurotically tied to them.

Another word for control is attachment. Ironically, the more we try to change or control someone, the more attached we become to that person. If your genuine wish is to divorce your parents and break your attachment to them, you must give up trying to control or change them.

### "My Mother Is Just a Witch": All-or-Nothing Thinking

Adult children of dysfunctional families have a tendency to think and act in extremes, seeing someone or something as either all good or all bad. There is no middle ground.

If you have a tendency to think this way, you may see your parent as all good or all bad instead of as someone with both good and bad qualities. Even though your parent may have hurt you tremendously and may be continuing to do so; even though she may be addicted to alcohol, drugs, gambling, or sex; and even though she may still be abusive to you, she is not *all bad*. She does have some good qualities; perhaps she is genuinely nice to others at times. While viewing her as all bad may make it easier for you to divorce her, it does not make it right. Understand that you are using this way of thinking as an excuse. Seeing your parent's good qualities will not sidetrack you from divorcing her if that is indeed what you need to do.

The following exercise will help you to counter all-or-nothing thinking:

List your parent's bad qualities.

Now, list her good qualities.

If you are unable to think of at least two good qualities in your parent, you are stuck in all-or-nothing thinking. Until you are able to have a somewhat more balanced view, you may question whether you are truly ready to divorce your parent.

In order to help you to think of some good qualities, try to remember at least one instance in your life when your parent was good to you. It may have been when you were a little baby, or perhaps since you became an adult. No matter how abusive, neglectful, or controlling your parent has been, there *have* been some good times, some loving moments. While this reality does not take away from the fact that your parent was abusive, it is important to recall those loving moments in order to bring your thinking into balance.

Although your parent may put on a false front for those outside the family, there may also be some truly good qualities that he or she exhibits to others but that you are not privy to. I remember resenting the fact that my mother seemed like two people: there was her "public self," who dressed beautifully, always carried herself well, and seemed so proud, and there was the mother *I* knew who came home each night, changed into old clothes, and proceeded to get drunk.

I always felt that she fooled other people, that they didn't know who she really was or what she was really like. In a way, that was true; there certainly was a tremendous discrepancy between her public and private selves. But much later on in my adulthood I became aware that there was a side to my mother I had never known. Over the years, she always had at least one close friend in addition to the friends she had at work. As I look back on it, people seemed to genuinely like her. As hard as it is for me to imagine, based on the way she has treated me, I think she must have been a good friend to those people.

Think of the way your parent is with other people. While it may make you feel even more angry to realize that he acts better toward outsiders than toward his own family, at least recognize this side of him. If you still feel stuck and cannot think of at least two good characteristics, ask others who know your parent. They may have information about him that you do not have that enables them to share something positive about him.

Rosemary's story is a good example of how all-or-nothing thinking can be a bad reason for divorcing a parent. Rosemary was raised by fundamentalist Christian parents who were extremely rigid, judgmental, perfectionistic, and punitive. If she didn't do as they wished, she would be punished severely, often in an abusive way. Her father beat her severely when she disobeyed him, and her mother would lock her in the cellar to "teach her a lesson" when she acted in a way that her mother deemed "unbecoming to a lady." She was not allowed to play with any children other than those in their church, and as a teenager she was not allowed to date, dance, wear makeup, or listen to the current music on the radio. Rosemary grew up to be an "all-or-nothing" thinker just like her parents, and so she viewed her parents as all bad.

When Rosemary first started therapy with me, she told me she hated her parents and wanted nothing to do with them ever again. She was unable to see any of their good qualities and had blocked out any memory of the positive aspects of her upbringing. In essence, she had become as rigid, judgmental, and perfectionistic as her parents.

Before Rosemary divorced her parents, I urged her to try to find some good memories about them and about her childhood, not as a way of diverting her from her righteous anger but as a way of bringing some balance into her thinking. She found it very difficult to do this. I encouraged her to release her emotions in constructive ways by writing her parents letters that she could choose to mail or not, and by talking out loud to them as if they were in the room. Once she was able to do this, her pain came flooding forth and with it her awareness that she did, indeed, still love them.

Once she was able to admit this to herself, she was also able to see some of her parents' good qualities, such as their good intentions and their genuine concern for her. Since she no longer saw them as all bad, she felt less afraid to be around them. She decided to try to spend a little more time with them and to try to look at them more objectively, both in terms of how willing they were to admit their mistakes in the past and how they treated her now. She found that they were willing to apologize to her for being abusive, and that they treated her with more respect now. For these reasons, she decided not to divorce them but to try again.

## YOU HAVE A CHOICE

Like Rosemary, you can change your mind at any time along the way as you begin to explore the possibility of divorcing a parent. You now know that you are not alone in your desire to divorce a parent, that you don't have to forgive, and that you do not have to continue to put up with abusive, neglectful, or controlling behavior from a parent. You know that you have a choice. You can choose to divorce from, temporarily separate from, or reconcile with one or both of your parents.

When you were a child you had few, if any, real choices. Adults controlled you and dictated your behavior. If you were unfortunate enough to be born into a dysfunctional family environment, you could do nothing about it. For better or worse, you were stuck until you got old enough to leave home. You could not change your parents, and you could not leave your parental home—after all, where would you go? No matter how bad your parents were, they were all you had. Your parents could get away with anything from beating you to neglecting your needs, and you could do nothing about it.

Unfortunately, some adults still feel trapped by their parents. Even though they are old enough to never see their parents again if they don't want to, they still feel bound by obligation, guilt, fear, or a misguided sense of loyalty. They are stuck, still feeling like children, still feeling that they have to go along with their parents' decisions and desires, still feeling that they have no choice. But they do have choices. As an adult, if you do not like what is happening in a particular situation or relationship, you can leave.

As radical as divorcing a parent may seem, it may sometimes be the only way to break out of the role of being a victim to your parent. If you have been waiting all your life for the day when you can escape from your parent's tyranny, there is no better time than the present. The chains that bind you are not as strong as you have been led to believe. If you use all your strength and all your will, you can break those chains and escape to a new life—one where you are not bound by your parent's desires,, demands, expectations, or rules, and where you can be free to become your real self. That self is not the person your parent wants you to be, but the person *you* want to be.

You don't have to forgive the unforgivable, you don't have to "live with" the unlivable, and you don't have to remain the captive of a parent who is tyrannical, controlling, critical, abusive, crazy-making, negating, or neglectful. You are free to do whatever you feel is best for you, including divorcing your parent.

CHAPTER **2**

# When Right Is on Your Side

There are many good reasons for divorcing a parent, some of which were discussed in the first chapter. In this chapter I'll explore some specific reasons for divorcing a parent, although obviously I cannot list every good reason that exists. Some of these reasons overlap, and you'll probably identify with at least one, if not several, of them.

## WHEN YOUR PARENT IS HYPERCRITICAL

When a parent is hypercritical, a child has absolutely no relief from criticism and can't do anything right. For some adult children, a parent's endless bickering with them, constant criticism, or continual attempts to control continue to chip away at their self-esteem and at their resolve to recover. These adult children may notice that each contact they have with their parents causes a setback in therapy or regression to an earlier stage of recovery.

This was the case with Jonathan:

> Each and every time I see my father or talk to him on the telephone, I end up questioning whether or not I should continue therapy. He'll say things to me like "How long are you going to stay in therapy? You've been going for two years now. Don't you think

that if it was going to do you any good, it would have by now? All those therapists want is to take your money. There's nothing wrong with you that a little hard work and a little discipline couldn't cure. You're just as lazy now as you ever were. When are you going to get a decent job and quit all this therapy stuff? It's just a waste of time."

Even though I've learned to defend myself somewhat with him and seem to hold my own against his accusations, I begin to doubt myself and my therapy because I sometimes don't see any progress myself. I'm still afraid to go out and get a better job because my self-esteem is so low, and I'm afraid I couldn't hold on to one if I got it. I still don't trust in my abilities.

After I've talked to my dad it takes me days, sometimes weeks, to snap myself out of my doubts and depression. I have to force myself to remember all the progress I've made in therapy and to remind myself that my self-esteem is so low because of the constant berating I received from my dad when I was growing up.

I remember trying to do my homework when I was a kid, feeling afraid that any moment my father would come into the room. Almost every night he'd come in, ask me how I was doing, and sit down next to me to watch me. I'd get so nervous with him watching like that that I would make mistakes. He'd be watching me so closely that of course he would catch the mistake and pull my ear sharply, saying, "Hey, what's this? That's not the right answer! Do that problem again!" Or, "You spelled that word wrong—correct it right now!"

Of course I'd be so nervous that I wouldn't be able to get the right answer or correct the spelling. Then he'd start to berate me. "You're so stupid! I can't believe you're my son! Where is your head? Don't you even bother to *think*?" He'd go at me for what would seem like hours but was probably only minutes. Then he would insist that I sit there until I got the right answer, even if it took all night.

I developed extreme anxiety in school whenever I had to take a test. I was so afraid of getting an answer wrong that I would sit paralyzed, unable to put down an answer. I was also terrified of standing up in front of the class to give a speech or book report. I imagined that the whole class was scrutinizing me like my dad did.

After several years in therapy and countless attempts at getting my dad to understand how his constant criticism was hurting me, I realized that the only way I was going to prevent myself from being continually damaged by my father was to stop having any contact with him. Otherwise I was doomed to failure.

Sandy described a different response to a hypercritical parent. After visiting her mother, she would binge on candy bars to the point that several times she passed out from too much sugar.

Whenever I used to leave my mother's, I couldn't wait to stuff my face with as many candy bars as I could stomach. I'd stop at the nearest store and buy handfuls of candy bars, dump them out of the bag on the empty seat next to me, and eat them the entire hour and a half it took to get home. I'd often get so sick that I would have to stop and throw up before I made it home. I know now that being around my mother made me feel self-hatred and self-loathing. Eating all those candy bars may have seemed like a child's way of rewarding herself, but in reality it was my way of *punishing* myself. That's the effect my mother always had on me. No matter how healthy I got, no matter how long I was able to abstain, I couldn't see her without becoming self-destructive. She was so critical and controlling, so emotionally abusive, that I always left feeling like a nothing. I felt I had to stop seeing her completely in order to maintain my physical and emotional health.

## WHEN YOUR PARENT IS MANIPULATIVE AND CONTROLLING

For years, Tony had been allowing his mother to manipulate him, even though he had been trying hard not to. He had expressed a lot of his anger toward her in his therapy sessions and had cut off most of his ties to her. He saw her only when absolutely necessary, and he told her little about his feelings. Even so, he still found himself being manipulated and controlled by her.

Every week, Tony's mother phoned him to invite him for Sunday dinner. She would say that she missed him and that Sundays were especially difficult for her without him. If he told her he had made other plans, she would become cold and hang up. But that was never the end of it. Later on in the week she would call him and tell her that she was very lonely, that no one ever visited her, and that she missed him terribly. Finally, out of guilt, he would give in to her.

After much therapy, Tony ultimately became better able to resist her ploys, and he felt quite proud of himself. But his mother wasn't about to give up.

One evening she called to tell him that she was desperately ill. It just so happened that Tony had a very important awards banquet to go to that night. But his mother really did sound sick, and when he asked her if she had called the doctor, she said that she thought she needed to be hospitalized. Tony went rushing over to her house, fully expecting to find her deathly ill. Instead, he found her all dressed up, with the table set for an elaborate meal. Tony was furious. "How could you lie to me like that?" he demanded. She told him that if she had to lie, she would—that she would do anything to get her son back. Tony stormed out of her house and hasn't been back since.

Unbeknownst to him it turned out that Tony was to receive an award that night, but he wasn't there to accept it. This seemed very symbolic to him: "All my life, my mother's needs came first. I really wish I could have accepted that award in person, but instead I was 'taking care of mother' again. I vowed it would be the last time.

## WHEN YOUR PARENT CONTINUES TO ABUSE YOU

When a parent continues to abuse you either verbally, physically, or sexually, and you are either unable to stand up for yourself or your attempts are not enough to stop the abuse, you may need to consider divorce.

Larry explained why he decided to divorce his father:

My dad is a very obnoxious man who always believes he is right. He loves to argue, and he has to have the last word on everything. When I was growing up he used to beat me into submission, but not that he can't do that (only because I'm bigger than he is) he tries to do it by intimidating me verbally. I do stand up for myself, but every time I do he becomes enraged and starts yelling and throwing things so it's as if he's still abusing me physically. I've tried not to argue with him, but he's the type of person who can argue by himself. I love my dad, but I just can't stand being around that kind of abuse any longer, so I've had to stop talking to him or seeing him.

Julie's attempts to deal with her father met with a similar result.

Even though I had confronted my father about his sexual abuse of me when I was a child, he continued to be sexually seductive with me. Whenever he looked at me it was like he was undressing me with his eyes, and he tried to give me a big wet kiss every time he saw me. I couldn't even stand next to him without his putting his arm around me and trying to touch my breast. On several occasions I warned him that if he didn't stop being sexual with me, I would have to stop seeing him, but he continued anyway. Finally, in order to save myself from further abuse and to stop allowing myself to be his victim, I had to stop seeing him.

## WHEN YOUR PARENT CONTINUES TO DENY THE TRUTH

Often, the reason parents do not stop their abusive behavior is that they are still in a state of denial. Denial is a defense mechanism that we all use at one time or another to cope with life. It enables us to block from our awareness certain information or emotions that we would otherwise have a difficult time facing. Without some healthy denial we could not tolerate the stresses, disappointments, and tragedies of life. Some people, however, have elaborately sophisticated denial systems that enable them to block out *any* unpleasant information or feelings. While in healthy individuals denial can serve as a temporary stopgap, a way of avoiding the truth until they are strong enough to handle it, in unhealthy individuals denial tends to be all-encompassing and more permanent. Such people find it impossible to face the truth, either because they feel very fragile and fear that they cannot handle it, or because they simply do not want to face the consequences.

Coming out of denial is an important step in the recovery process for adult children. Unless they face the truth about their childhoods, including the truth about their parents, they cannot fully recover. Because the truth becomes so important to adult children, they become particularly offended by denial and dishonesty. Geneva told me, "As long as my mother continues to say that she didn't physically abuse me, I feel negated by her. As a part of my recovery, I need to have the abuse acknowledged. If she cannot admit to what she did and how it affected me, then to be around her is to be living a lie."

Some adult children cannot continue to be around parents who are still strongly in denial, because it confuses them and causes them to doubt their own perceptions about their parents and about their childhoods. Sometimes a parent's denial is so strong and so contagious that the adult child goes back into denial in his presence.

This was Cynthia's problem.

My father refuses to admit that he sexually abused me when I was a child. I don't know for certain if my mother has ever believed me, but she acts as if it didn't happen, either. Whenever I go over there I end up feeling nuts, because everyone acts as though nothing ever happened. When I talk about some of the difficulties I have with men, they act like they don't understand what it's all about. The other day Mother had the nerve to say to me, "You know, I think it's because you matured so late—I guess you just never caught up to the other girls."

As crazy as it may seem, when I'm at their house I start to doubt that anything did happen! They act so normal now—they seem so happy, and they're both so nice to me. I know there's a part of me that wishes that the fantasy was true, that I could pretend it all away like they have. But days or weeks later, after my therapist and other group members have reminded me of what really happened to me, I come out of my "denial stupor" and feel really angry. I feel angry that they continue to lie to me and to themselves like that, and I feel angry that I allowed them to pull the wool over my eyes one more time. I especially feel angry because of all the wasted time I have to spend coming back to the truth!

## BREAKING THE CYCLE OF ABUSE

One of the many consequences of denial is that it enables people to continue their abusive behavior. For generations, parents have been abusing their children, and these abused children in turn often grow up to abuse their own children. Because of our increased knowledge about abusive and dysfunctional families, we are the first generation to be able to break this cycle and ensure that we do not pass on this legacy of abuse.

When Eric was a child, his father used to beat him mercilessly. His mother ignored it, and Eric never told anyone else about it, so in some ways it seemed to him as though nothing had ever really happened. He thought he had survived it well enough, but then he started repeating the cycle of abuse with his own children. Whenever he'd been around his father he would come home and become very abusive to his children and his wife. She finally left him over it. Eric admitted to his group, "I have to say I respected her for it. At least she didn't stand by helplessly like my mother did. When she left, she told me that the only way she was going to allow me to see the kids was if I stopped seeing my dad and got into therapy. The court upheld her request. I desperately wanted to see my kids, so I reluctantly went into therapy and even more reluctantly stopped seeing my dad." He went on:

I realized several things while I was in therapy. First of all, I noticed that the longer I stayed away from my father, the less agitated I felt. I realized that whenever I was around him I would feel the old feelings come back that I had felt as a child. I was still afraid of him, so I tended to tiptoe around him, but I also felt enraged at him for beating me as a child. Of course, I couldn't let him know about it. He still yelled and swore when things didn't go his way, just as he had when I was a child. I don't think I was ever sure that he wouldn't hit me if I crossed him, and I sure didn't want to find out. Instead of letting him know about my anger—or letting myself know, for that matter—I would go home and let all that anger out on my wife and kids. I was acting just like my dad!

In therapy, I finally recognized that I hate my dad. I hate him for abusing me, but I hate him even more for being such a terrible role model. He couldn't stand up to his boss at work, so he took his anger out on me. I couldn't stand up to *him*, so I abused my own kids.

I still see my mother once in a while, although I realize I resent her as well. But at least I'm not afraid to tell her about my anger toward her. I don't ever see or speak to my father, and it feels good. I can't get my wife back, but I do have visitation rights now that there is no danger of my abusing my kids. They're in therapy now, and I encourage them to get angry with me for having been abusive to them when they were younger. I truly hope that the cycle of abuse stops with them.

Many adult children become increasingly concerned that their children will be negatively affected by being around their grandparents. This is a valid concern if one or both of your parents were abusive to you. Unless your parents have acknowledged their abusive behavior, received psychological help for their problems, or joined a support group that focuses on recovery from their problems (such as Parents Anonymous, Parents United, or Alcoholics Anonymous), they are very likely to continue to be abusive, not only to you but to your children as well.

Adrienne couldn't trust her father with her children.

He had sexually abused me, my sisters, my brother, and my cousin. And even though my mother said she would never leave my kids alone with him, I couldn't trust her to protect them from him. Once when I came to pick them up, I found my father sitting in the living room watching television with my kids. I found my mother lying down taking a nap, the same thing she used to do while my father molested me!

I stopped leaving my kids with them after that, but pretty soon I didn't even feel comfortable having them in his presence at all. I know how little time it takes to molest a child, and it was impossible to follow them everywhere—into the bathroom, out into the backyard, into the garage. I felt like a nervous wreck trying to watch the kids all the time, and it was making them nervous, too, to have me watching them so closely.

My husband and I started visiting my parents without the kids for a while, but I soon realized that I just didn't want to be around people I couldn't trust. I had begged my mother to leave my father several times and she had refused, so I knew that was hopeless. Finally, I came to the conclusion that it was best for all concerned if we just stopped seeing one another. It's funny, but my parents didn't put up that much of a fuss about it. I wonder if they were both relieved about not having to risk abusing the kids and not having to deal with me about my abuse.

As harsh as it may sound, the only way to guarantee that your children won't be abused by the people who abused you is to make sure they are never around them. Experts in the field of child abuse know that a person who is capable of abusing one child is very likely to abuse others as well unless he receives help. The following letter was written to *Child* magazine:

> I am from a family with an extremely abusive mother. I am a mother myself now, and it is painful for me to raise my child because I have to recall in detail the abuse I endured so that I do not repeat with my child what my mother did to me. Every move I make seems to be guarded, and I feel it is taking much of the joy and spontaneity from the relationship I have with my child, but I am determined to break the cycle of abuse. I want to raise my child to be a loving and kind person with high self-esteem. I broke relations with my mother over ten years ago, when I finally realized that she is still as abusive as she ever was. I will never expose my child to her because I will not allow her to abuse my child the way she abused me. . . .

## CHOOSING SOBRIETY OR ABSTINENCE OVER YOUR PARENTS

Recovering alcoholics or addicts frequently have setbacks after seeing their parents, often because their parents themselves are alcoholics or addicts. For this reason, many such adult children choose to stay away from their parents, choosing their sobriety instead.

Rachel shared her story with her AA group:

> I went over to my parents' house on Sunday for my sister's birthday party. As usual, everyone was drinking. Even though I felt uncomfortable being around the alcohol, it didn't bother me too much for a while. But then my mother started getting drunk and obnoxious, and I just couldn't stand it. The memories of all my birthday parties when my mother would get sloppy drunk and embarrass me in front of my friends came flooding back. I just couldn't handle my rage. I felt like screaming at her at the top of my lungs and grabbing her and shaking her sober. But instead I just quietly left, drove my car

to the nearest liquor store, went home, and got drunk for the first time in two years.

Tom had a similar story.

My whole family and all their friends drink. Whenever I go over there they put such a tremendous amount of pressure on me to drink that it's unreal. I feel so uncomfortable with the pressure that for now I have to stay away in order to maintain my sobriety.

These adult children don't blame their parents, for their addictions or for their slips. Instead, they recognize that they simply aren't strong enough yet to be around their parents without risking their sobriety. If this is your situation, you might consider temporarily separating from your parent instead of permanently divorcing him or her. Eventually, as you get stronger and have more time being abstinent, you may find that you can be around your parent again. On the other hand, as you become healthier you may also become less willing to be around alcohol or drug abusers.

## BREAKING THE CODEPENDENCY HABIT

Adult children from abusive families often remain neurotically tied to a parent because they have taken on the role of the "rescuer" or "caretaker." Whether the parent is an alcoholic, a drug addict, a battered wife or a batterer, a compulsive gambler, or a sex addict, they try to change their parent's behavior and thus save her from herself. This behavior, called codependence, is now considered to be a disease itself.

A broader definition of codependency is given by Sharon Wegscheider-Cruse:

Codependency is a specific condition that is characterized by preoccupation and extreme dependence (emotionally, socially, and sometimes physically) on a person or object. Eventually, this dependence on another person becomes a pathological condition that affects the codependent in all other relationships.

In addition, codependency is a pattern of dependence on approval from others in an attempt to find safety, self-worth, and identity. Codependents can become so obsessed with getting others to approve of them that in their frustration they may become work-aholics, alcoholics, shopaholics, drug addicts, sex addicts, food abusers, or compulsive gamblers.

Although any caring person feels the pain of a loved one who is suffering, codependents feel an excessive, unhealthy identification with a loved one's pain. Some adult children are more comfortable attending to their parents' problems than to their own. This consuming caretaking shields them from facing their own issues. Some adult children are so attached to their parents that the relationship is like an addiction.

Sometimes, divorcing a parent may be the only way of making sure that you do not continue to try to rescue or control your parent. Donna described the situation that finally caused her to decide to divorce both of her parents:

> I started realizing that both my mother and father were going down the tubes. Their alcoholism had progressed to such an extent that their behavior was getting more and more bizarre. They were so damaged and so sick that I could not help them. Each time I tried to, I got pulled into the quicksand and started going down with them. I'd try to rescue them from some situation they'd gotten themselves into, and I'd end up putting my own life in jeopardy. I'd find myself in such dangerous places in the middle of the night that I'm surprised I'm alive! I finally realized I had to let go—I wasn't helping them, and I certainly wasn't helping myself. I was just avoiding my own problems and getting deeper and deeper into codependency.

Audrey loved her father very much, and because of this she didn't want to have to divorce him. But he was making a mess out of his own life and was making her life miserable.

> I can't tell you how often I felt like a fool for getting sucked into one more of my father's lies. For years he would come to me with some story about how he needed money for an emergency—to fix his car

so he could go to work, to go to the dentist because he was in such pain, to pay a bill to avoid collection. And each time I would later find out that he had used the money to buy booze and go on a binge. It seemed like I just never learned. Even though I couldn't trust him, I always worried that maybe this time he was telling me the truth, and I knew I couldn't live with myself if he really needed the money.

Things got so bad that he started breaking into my house and stealing from me, or I would come home to find him passed out in my front yard or asleep in his car in my driveway. I felt so ashamed for my neighbors to see my father like that, and so enraged with him for putting me in such a position. His health was rapidly declining, but he refused to go to Alcoholics Anonymous or enter a treatment program, even when the doctor told him that if he didn't stop drinking his liver would fail completely and he would die. I felt sorry for him, because I knew he had a disease, but since he refused to get help I knew it would be only a matter of time before he bottomed out completely.

In the meantime, I decided I couldn't allow him to take me with him on his destructive journey. I wrote him a letter telling him that I didn't want to see him anymore and wanted him to stay away from my house. He kept calling and coming over, so I finally filed a restraining order with the police to keep him away. I haven't heard from him since he was notified of the restraining order, and I don't know how he is doing. I worry about him sometimes, but mostly I have just given him up to the alcohol.

## WHEN IT'S EITHER YOU OR THEM

As I've revealed, it was necessary for me to divorce my mother in order to save my health. Many other adult children have had to divorce their parents in order to literally save their lives.

When Lorena first went into therapy, her therapist took one look at her and asked, "Who is killing you?" As unusual as this question was, it turned out to be very appropriate, because Lorena's spirit was indeed slowly being killed by her mother's cruelty. Her mother deliberately made Lorena doubt her abilities and managed to take away or sabotage everything positive in Lorena's life. Although she would tell Lorena to her face that she was her favorite child, she would complain about her behind her back, often turning other people against her. Whenever Lorena, an extremely attractive young woman, would get attention for her beauty, her mother would appear to be proud of her in front of other people but would cut her down when they were alone together. While she would bask in the attention she got for being Lorena's mother, she was extremely jealous of Lorena and was constantly competing with her.

In a clear case of the pot calling the kettle black, Lorena's mother once went after her with a butcher knife because she imagined Lorena was thinking negative thoughts about her. This occurred when Lorena was 25, during one of the rare times when the entire family got together. They were all having dinner, and things had seemed to be going just fine, when out of the blue Lorena's mother glared at her and said, "I heard that. I heard what you just said about me." Lorena, stunned, said, "I didn't say anything." But her mother insisted, "Oh, yes, you did. I heard you!"—at which point she stormed out of the room, returning in a few moments with a butcher knife. She started toward Lorena in a rage, and she would have stabbed her had she not been restrained by several family members. That was the last straw, as far as Lorena was concerned—and that was the last time she ever saw her mother.

## WHEN YOUR PARENT WON'T ACCEPT YOUR LIFESTYLE

Even though Andrew had come out to his mother three years ago, she could not accept the fact that he was gay. Even after she had agreed to go to a few meetings of the support group Mothers of Gays, she remained in denial, still talking to Andrew as though he were straight. While he was always invited to family gatherings, his lover of five years, Tom, was never invited. Holidays were especially difficult for Andrew, since if he wanted to be with his parents he couldn't be with Tom. This went on for several years, until finally Andrew decided he couldn't stand it any longer.

When his mother invited him for Thanksgiving, he asked whether Tom could come, too. His mother responded, "Oh, no, that wouldn't be appropriate at all." When Andrew asked why not, he was told that Thanksgiving was for family only.

"But what about my brothers' wives? Why are they allowed to come?"

"Of course their wives can come—they're part of the family now, aren't they?"

"Well, what about Leonard's girlfriends—why is he always allowed to bring whomever he is seeing?" That silenced his mother for a moment. Then Andrew tried to explain. "Listen, mother, I've been with Tom for five years now. It's as if we *are* married."

Finally, his mother blurted out, "It *isn't* the same, and you can never convince me that it is! It disgusts me to think of you with a man, and no matter how much you try to convince me that it's normal and natural, I will never believe it."

Andrew's feelings were very hurt. He had not realized his mother felt this way. He was now aware of the fact that she not only would not accept his relationship with Tom, but that she would never accept *him*. Sadly, Andrew had to divorce his mother in order to stand up for his belief that he was not a perverted person.

## NEEDING TO SEPARATE

Adult children from dysfunctional families have a difficult time growing up and separating from their parents. This is true for several reasons, the most significant of which is that they often continue to try to get the love, attention, and approval that they never received as children. This drive to get unmet needs met is extremely strong, and it can sometimes overshadow all other needs.

Abused children will put up with almost any behavior from a parent in order to get some attention. They are quick to forgive and forget as soon as the parent gives them any positive attention. Even children who are so severely beaten that social-service agencies are called in will frequently deny any charges of abuse on a parent's part as a way of protecting the parent. They do this because they are afraid of the parent and of losing the parent, and because they want to please the parent.

There are certain emotional building blocks (nurturing, caring, and support) that all children need to get from their parents in order to grow up to be independent individuals. If you were deprived of some of these, you probably feel incomplete and inadequate. Unfortunately, this need to get now what you missed out on then keeps you tied to your parents in a very negative way. You may feel "lacking" and "incomplete" and want your parents to finish up the job they started. This unhealthy tie can sometimes be broken only by divorce.

## "It's About Time I Grew Up"

You might ask, "Can't the adult child just accept the fact that he needs to grow up, without involving the parent? Why is divorce necessary?" To answer this question, it is necessary to understand some basics of child development.

The bond between a mother and a child who is loved, nurtured, and protected is extremely strong and deep. Not all mothers are able to establish emotional bonds with their children; ironically, these children seem to attach themselves even more strongly to their mothers than do children who are nurtured. Without this bonding and the accompanying nurturing and unconditional love, the child feels incomplete. He feels that if only he could get his mother's love he could grow up and become an independent adult.

The sad part of this is that the adult child obviously cannot go back and get what he didn't get as a child. It is too late. He will just have to grow up without it. Oftentimes, this growing up occurs only when there is a permanent separation from the mother.

When I met Sally, she wore frilly dresses and had ribbons in her hair, and her high-pitched, little-girl voice belied her almost 29 years. Even though she lived on her own, Sally was still tied to her mother. She spoke with her mother almost daily and went over to her house at least three times a week. As a child, she had compensated for her mother's neglect and lack of affection by taking on the role of the good little girl, a role she continued to play even as an adult. She was constantly trying to please her mother by running her errands and cooking meals for her, taking her to the movies, and cleaning her house. But her mother complained about the way Sally cooked, never liked the movies they saw, and focused on all that Sally *hadn't* done.

Sally was so busy trying to please her mother that she didn't have time for her own life. She stayed in a dead-end job because she didn't have time to go to night school to better herself. "After all," she said to me, "how can I go to school when I have to take Mother to her bingo game on Monday and run errands for her the rest of the week? There just aren't enough hours in the day!" She also didn't have time to date. "Once in a while I have a date on a Saturday night, but my weekends are so full of things I have to do with Mother that I can't go out very often. Once I start dating a man steadily he seems to want a lot of my time, and I just don't have it!"

Besides finally becoming aware that she was stuck in the good-little-girl role, Sally also realized that her self-esteem was constantly being undermined by a mother she would never be able to please, no matter what she did. She tried cutting back and not doing as much for her mother, but this caused her mother to become more critical and even belligerent. Time after time Sally tried to explain to her mother why she was spending less time with her, but her mother refused to understand. This put Sally in a terrible bind: she longed very much for her mother's approval and love, but she knew that it was time to grow up. No matter how hard she tried, whenever she was around her mother she slipped back into the role of the good little girl, and she would then feel terrible about herself afterwards. Eventually, Sally came to the painful conclusion that she must stop seeing her mother in order to grow up.

Sally has been very happy with her decision. She is now enrolled in night school and is studying to be a legal secretary and she has been dating the same man for five months. Her little-girl voice has matured, and the frilly, childish dresses she used to wear have been replaced by more appropriate adult clothes.

Christina Crawford's book *Mommie Dearest* gave us a good example of a child who thought she could win her mother's love in spite of the mother's continual cruelty. Christina explained that she should have learned to stop trying to gain her mother's love and approval, since each attempt was met with rejection and cruelty. But her need for the love she had never received as a child was such a strong motivating force that she continued to seek her mother's approval right up until her mother died. Even then her mother got the last word, leaving nothing to Christina in her will. Had she been able to divorce herself from her mother earlier on, she could have spared herself years of agony and pain, since her mother was incapable of loving her.

No matter how futile their attempts might be, some adult children continue to look for any sign of love and approval on a parent's part, even when there are never any such signs. They continue to harbor the false hope that someday the parent will change, thinking that perhaps if they wait long enough, change enough, or forgive enough, they will receive the love they crave. No matter how many times they are rejected or how hard they try to give up the false hope, some adult children continue to try in spite of themselves.

Some adult children finally realize that divorcing the parent is the only way out of a very negative pattern, one that keeps them stuck where they are and prevents any further growth. This was the case with Erin.

Erin had been treated poorly by her mother her entire life. Her mother made it clear that she preferred Erin's sister, Carol, who was prettier and more popular. But Erin never gave up trying to win her mother's love, which was especially important to her because her father had died when she was 6 years old. She tried hard in school, never got into any trouble, and helped out around the house—things Carol didn't do.

When Carol graduated from high school, she was given a new car. When Erin graduated, she got a new dress. When her sister got married, her mother paid for the wedding. When Erin got married, her mother told her she didn't have enough money. Erin tried to ignore her mother's obvious preference. She continued to always be the one who would listen to her mother's problems and who would run errands and do other favors for her.

It wasn't until Erin's first child was born prematurely that she was finally able to face the fact that her mother did not care about her. Her mother, who had doted on her sister's three children, only came to the hospital once, when Erin's baby was first born. Although the child was in intensive care for several weeks, Erin did not see or hear from her mother during that time. When she finally confronted her mother about it, her mother told her that she had been too busy baby-sitting Carol's children to come to the hospital. For Erin, this was the final blow.

"I was always just an obligation to her, anyway," she told me. "She didn't even notice I had stopped speaking to her until she hadn't heard from me in over three months. Then she called 'to find out how I was,' as if nothing had happened. When I was cold to her, she acted insulted and has not called back. I am so unimportant to her that she hasn't even tried to find out what's wrong."

### The Special Problems of Sexual Abuse

A child who is introduced to adult sexuality at an early age, before he or she is emotionally and physiologically equipped to handle it, will likely also have problems with separation and self-identity. An incestuous father, for example, assaults his daughter's separateness by saying, in effect, "You are mine to do with as I will." At the same time, he is also forcing on her a premature separateness from parental nurturing and protection by also saying, "You are not my daughter, you are my lover." Growing up and separating is difficult enough: when there is sexual abuse, the process is confounded and becomes much harder. Thus, connectedness becomes fusion, intimacy becomes intrusion.

Sexual abuse sometimes causes a child to merge psychologically with the parent in a very unhealthy way. Some victims have felt "married" to their fathers or mothers because of the sexual merging. If the father has intercourse with the child there is also a physical merging of their two bodies, further increasing the difficulty of separation. During the act of intercourse, there is an emotional and psychological merging and meshing that occurs. This illusionary feeling of "oneness," while being a romantic notion with adult lovers, can cause a child to regress back to earlier stages of development, when oneness was a more natural experience with parents.

Carolyn, who still lived at home with her parents, was 22 when she initially entered therapy because of her nonexistent social life. "I just don't understand it," she said. "I can find myself attracted to a man, but when he asks me out, all I can do is think of my dad and how he'd feel. I would feel, I don't know . . . kind of disloyal to my dad."

After many months of therapy, Carolyn was finally able to tell me about her father's sexual abuse, which had begun when she was 13. It took her much longer to realize why it was that she felt so unwilling to date. Finally, she was able to make the connection: "No wonder I feel guilty about dating other men—I feel married to my father!" She became aware that ever since her father had started having intercourse with her, she had thought of him as her husband. He treated her like his wife in many other ways as well, confiding in her about his problems at work, having her iron his shirts and make him coffee. Carolyn began to realize that she was tied to her father in a very unhealthy way.

It wasn't long afterward that she decided to move out of her parents' house. Her father became very upset, and in a heated argument he accused her of wanting to move out so she could have affairs with men. Enraged by her new awareness of how his sexual abuse had damaged her, she yelled at him, "Yes, Dad, I do want to have sex with other men! Did you think *you* were going to be the only man who ever had me?" At this point his father struck her across the face. Carolyn moved out that night.

She has only seen her father once since then, at her mother's funeral three years ago. After her father had begun to sexually abuse her, Carolyn withdrew from her mother, both out of guilt and because she felt competitive with her. Because she had strongly suspected that her mother knew about the incest all along, and because she had stayed married to Carolyn's father even after Carolyn told her of the sexual abuse, Carolyn had never become close to her mother. But she never stopped loving her mother, and her death hit her hard. When she saw her father at the funeral, all her feelings of anger toward him melted away, and she reached up to hug him. As he hugged her, he drew his body close to hers in a very sexual way. Appalled, she pushed him away and said, "I see you haven't changed!"

"Yeah, and you haven't either," he snarled. "I hear you're still a whore!"

Devastated, Carolyn walked away from him once and for all.

As in Carolyn's case, sexual abuse by a father or stepfather frequently causes the female child to feel alienated and estranged from her mother. The child may feel guilty, or she may be afraid that her mother will reject her. Often, the father has deliberately turned the child against her mother in order to insure her silence and her loyalty to him. The sexual abuse thus causes a premature, unnatural pseudo-separation of the daughter from the mother.

When Jennifer's father started sexually abusing her when she was seven years old, she immediately felt more distant from her mother. Confused by Jennifer's sudden distance, her mother tried to reach out to her, but to no avail. Jennifer's father had told the child that he was unhappy because her mother never paid enough attention to him. He told her he was going to teach her to be a good wife so that she wouldn't ignore her husband's sexual needs the way her mother did. Jennifer felt that if her mother had been a good wife, she wouldn't have to do these things with her father. She also felt guilty and ashamed about what her father was doing to her, and she was afraid her mother would not love her if she found out. As the years went by, she became more and more distant from her mother.

Because of the sexual abuse by her father, Jennifer was deprived of the mothering and nurturing she needed as a child. Now, at 34, she is still neurotically attached to her mother. They are constantly fighting. Jennifer has told her mother about the sexual abuse she endured for years, and she blames her for not stopping it and for abdicating her responsibilities as a wife. Her mother feels so accused by Jennifer that she is unwilling to give her the nurturing Jennifer feels she still needs. They are both stuck.

Jennifer's mother does feel guilty for not having protected her daughter better (although she denies this to Jennifer), so she sometimes tolerates abusive behavior from Jennifer. Jennifer is caught between her desire to get the nurturing from her mother she never got and her anger toward her for not having been a better mother. If there is a chance for this relationship, Jennifer will need to accept the fact that she will never get from her mother what she needed as a child, and she will have to stop blaming her mother for her father's actions. For her part, Jennifer's mother will need to try to get past her guilt feelings and to be as loving a mother as she can now. Otherwise, the two may need to separate temporarily in order to get unstuck and to gain some empathy for each other's position.

### "They Won't Let Me Go"

Some parents simply will not *allow* their adult children to separate in a healthy way. Parents hold onto their children by:

- ☐ encouraging them to remain children
- ☐ making them feel incompetent and inadequate
- ☐ giving them too much, so they don't have to work to get things on their own
- ☐ causing them to be too fearful
- ☐ becoming sexually involved with their children
- ☐ criticizing all of their children's friends and dates, and thereby making them think that no one is good enough
- ☐ being "too good" a mother, not allowing children to feel any frustration and thus learn ways to solve their own problems

Why do parents try to hold on to their children? There are three primary reasons:

1. Separation reduces their power and control.
2. Separation makes them feel less needed, less important.
3. They are afraid for their children.

Darla's friend Crystal didn't understand her. "Darla's parents bought her a condominium and they send her money any time she needs it, but she complains because they call her on the phone too much! My parents don't *ever* call me, much less buy me condos or give me money. She seems so ungrateful!"

No one looking in from the outside could understand how tortured Darla was about her relationship with her parents. From all outward appearances, they certainly seemed to be extremely concerned about her. But Darla was being smothered by them. They dictated where she lived, when she should buy clothes, where she should go on vacation, and where she worked. They came over to her house unannounced. Worst of all they had taken her son away from her.

When Darla was 20 years old she had become pregnant, but her boyfriend had refused to marry her. Already living on her own, she had decided to keep the baby. With her parents' encouragement, she had moved back home so her parents could baby-sit while she worked. Darla had felt very lucky that her parents would help her like this, until she began to realize that they were treating her baby as if he were theirs. It bothered her to see them doting over him, but she told herself that she was just jealous because they had never given her that kind of attention. Eventually, she realized that her son saw her more as a big sister than as his mother. Her parents did so much for him and spent so much time with him that she just couldn't compete.

Darla moved out on her own again when her son was 10. But even then her parents often convinced her to leave her son at their house for the weekend, reasoning with her that she should be able to have a social life.

It wasn't until Darla entered therapy at 43 that she came to realize how much she resented her parents for having taken her son from her. Her parents were supporting her son while he went to college and he was very close to them, calling them far more than he ever called her. She regretted very much not having a closer relationship with her son, but even more than this the fact that her parents now controlled him just as they had always controlled her. Since her parents held the purse strings, her son felt that he had to consult with them about which school to go to and which classes he was going to take.

Darla's parents had created a "tender trap" for her son, just as they had for her—maintaining control over him through his finances, making him comfortable but dependent. Like Darla's parents, many parents use money as a means of emotional blackmail, controlling and manipulating their children long after they leave the nest. Some dangle the carrot of an inheritance when they die to intimidate and control their children while they are still alive.

The longer Darla was in therapy, the healthier she became and the more she tried to stand up to her parents and not allow them to dictate her life. She was appalled when she realized that her parents had not only stunted her own emotional growth but were now preventing her son from growing up as well. She worried that he would never become an independent adult.

When her son graduated from college, Darla breathed a sigh of relief, thinking that now he would be on his own and would stop depending on her parents for financial support. But instead of getting a job he managed to get even more money from her parents as an investment in a business deal of his. Although Darla hated to admit it, she realized that her son was going to milk her parents for all he could get. Why should he work when they would support him indefinitely? They had an investment in keeping him dependent, just as they had had with Darla, and he was willing to pay the price.

Some adult children find it impossible to be independent, autonomous adults while they are connected in any way to their parents. Try as they may, they revert back to unhealthy, childlike patterns of behavior whenever they are around them. This was Darla's situation. In time she realized that she needed to sever all ties with her parents, including buying them out of the condo, in order to break her dependence on them.

## WHEN IT'S JUST TOO LATE

Sometimes adult children have experienced such tremendous pain at the hands of a parent that continuing the relationship is impossible. Try as they may, they cannot forgive, they cannot forget, and they cannot regain the trust necessary for a healthy, close relationship.

Many adult children whose parents have sexually abused them find it impossible to continue the relationship. This is not just because it is difficult to forgive a parent for such a devastating act, but also because being around the parent is often terribly uncomfortable. Of course, if sexual abuse is still occurring, it is easy to understand why the adult child would prefer not to be in the parent's company. But many adult children feel this way even when the abuse has stopped. Why is this?

The most significant reason is that when a parent sexually abuses a child, he or she betrays that child's trust. This trust is a very hard thing to ever recover, as Wanda found:

> I was so devastated when I was a child by being sexually abused by my father that I now feel edgy with him and half expect him to try something again, even though he never does. There is just no basis for a relationship if the trust isn't there.

Nicki's experience was similar:

> I found that whenever I tried to be around my father I would experience a lot of discomfort. He was uncomfortable, too. For a long time we both tried to pretend that it had never happened, but it just didn't work. Then I thought that if we talked about it openly it might make it easier to be around each other. But that made him feel even more uncomfortable—he was just too embarrassed. I think we both feel more comfortable not being around each other.

Sexual abuse is not the only behavior that can destroy trust permanently. Often a parent's alcohol abuse can make it just as difficult for the child to trust the parent again. Dan's father is a recovering alcoholic with two years of sobriety, but Dan is still finding it hard to establish a healthy trusting relationship with him.

> Even though my dad is sober now, I'm still waiting for him to slip. When I was a kid he would periodically stop drinking for a while, but he would always start again if things got tough. Now I find I

watch him like a hawk, especially if he's under stress, just waiting for him to take that first drink.

My dad is a really nice guy now that he isn't drinking, but he hurt me so much and in so many ways when I was a kid. He used to become a wild man, throwing things at me if I crossed him. He hit me with a lamp once, and I landed in the hospital for several weeks with a severe concussion. Now when I'm around him, I always feel like I have to get ready to duck if he gets angry. I know he would probably never hurt me now that he is sober, but it's as if the child part of me just can't trust it. I get so nervous being around him that I'm miserable.

I also find that my memories of the things he used to do still keep coming up, and this interferes with the way I see him now. I can be sitting having a good conversation with him, only to be shaken by a flashback of when he would stand over me and beat me viciously with his fists, or of the times he used to slam me against the wall. I'm just not sure I can be around him with the tremendous fear I still feel.

You may have some reasons of your own for divorcing your parent that aren't on my list. As long as your motive is not to punish, teach a lesson, or try to change or manipulate your parent, and as long as you are operating out of love and caring for yourself, your reasons are probably good ones. The chapter that follows will help you to take the next step: that of deciding whether or not to divorce your parents.

# CHAPTER 3

# Is Divorce the Healthy Choice for You?

Even though you may have excellent reasons for divorcing your parent and would feel justified in doing so, you may still be unable to make a decision. Nagging doubts may haunt you, strong emotions may scare you, and pressure from others may confuse you.

Only you can make the decision to divorce a parent. No one should be allowed to pressure you by trying to talk you into or out of it. Suzy shared how she felt pressured by several members of her incest survivors group:

> Many of the women had divorced their fathers, and I felt pressure from them to do the same. But I didn't feel as they did. I had a lot of anger toward my father for molesting me, but I still loved him and wanted him in my life. I got so that I felt uncomfortable sharing in the group because they seemed to feel so differently about their fathers.

Margot's experience was just the opposite. She wanted to divorce herself from both of her parents, but she felt pressured by church members to forgive them and to continue the relationship.

> The people at my church just don't understand how very cruel and destructive my parents were to me. They believe that I should

51

forgive them and continue to see them, but I just can't. I've tried to explain to these people that my parents allowed their friends to molest me, and that they would have wild parties where my parents and their friends would all be naked and taking drugs, but they just tell me that I should forgive my parents, that they need my help and my prayers—that they need me to preach the Lord to them. They just don't understand—I *can't* be around my parents!

Making the decision of whether or not to divorce a parent can cause you much agonizing and deliberation, and there may be seemingly endless attempts at reconciliation. Many years of pain, anger, fear, and guilt may precede your decision. Sometimes it can only be made following much compromise and humiliation.

No one should make this type of life-changing decision without a great deal of soul-searching. You need to keep trying until you feel there is absolutely no hope. For example, you must try every possible way to communicate to your parent that his behavior has hurt you or continues to hurt you, and why. Surprisingly, parents are often oblivious to the fact that they are hurting their adult children with their abusive behavior. This doesn't excuse their behavior, nor does it excuse the fact that they are so oblivious to others' feelings, but it may explain how they can continue hurting their children without seeming to care. You need to work on learning to communicate with your parents in a clear, honest way so that you can let them know what your needs are and what kinds of behavior you are willing and not willing to accept.

The exercises in this chapter are designed to help you decide whether you want and need to divorce your parent—not whether you should or shouldn't. We will begin this process by exposing your denial. In order to come to a clear decision, you will need to work past your denial about how abusive, neglectful, critical, or controlling your parent was or is, and take an honest look both at who she has been to you and who she is now. The former is accomplished by reviewing your childhood and recalling how your parent mistreated you. You will then be instructed to notice how your parent treats you *now* and to list what she currently does that upsets you.

Once you have clarified these two areas, you will need to find constructive ways of releasing your anger regarding her mistreatment so that you do not divorce your parent out of anger or retaliation (a list of anger-releasing techniques will be provided).

It is easy to get caught up in doing what we think we *should* do—that is, what others expect us to do, or what we think is the "right" thing to do. Most people you know are not going to think divorcing your parent is the right thing for you to do. And yet, what about what you *want?* Make sure you do what is best for you, instead of what others think is right for you. There are no "shoulds" when it comes to this issue, only wants and needs.

In this chapter you will explore two ways of discovering what you really want. One is to listen to your inner voice, and the other is to listen to your body's messages. You will learn how to connect with your inner voice and how to listen to its words of wisdom when you ask yourself whether divorce is the healthy choice for you. You will also begin to pay attention to how your body reacts when you are around your parents, and you will learn to respect its messages.

If you are contemplating divorcing both parents, you will need to address each parent separately when you do the exercises.

## REVIEWING YOUR PAST

It is important to face the truth about your parents. While some adult children see their parents as all bad, as we discusssed in chapter 1, many people from dysfunctional families tend to deny how bad their childhoods really were and how much they were hurt by their parents. This is especially true at the beginning of recovery. One of the biggest obstacles to facing the truth is our tendency to make our parents better than they really are and to excuse their abusive behavior. Writing your story down will be of particular benefit, since once it is in black and white, it will be a constant reminder of what you have been through and will be harder for you to deny.

On a piece of paper or in a notebook or journal, list every abusive incident and every act of neglect or abandonment that your parent ever did to you, beginning as far back as you can remember.

Here is an excerpt from my own list:

1. When I was a very little girl (under three) my mother used to let me roam freely in the neighborhood while she slept. I could have been abducted by someone or hit by a car, since we lived on a busy street.

2. When I was six, she beat me with a switch because she forgot that I had told her where I would be.

3. One time, she sent me to the store and I lost the quarter she had given me to buy some tuna. I went home and told her I had dropped the money, but she didn't believe me; she thought I had spent it. She angrily took me back to the store and asked the storekeeper if I had bought any candy with the money. He told her no, that I had dropped it and we hadn't been able to get it from under the counter.

4. I once got a beating for lying because I told her the baby-sitter was critical of her. She confronted the baby-sitter, who of course lied and said she hadn't said those things.

5. She used to get drunk and become verbally abusive, telling me what a selfish, no-good kid I was. She would get so drunk that she'd fall down.

6. She didn't teach me how to brush my teeth, tie my shoes, or change my underwear. She'd spend hours getting herself ready to go someplace, and yet she would send me off to school looking like a ragamuffin.

7. She was critical of all my friends. I got the feeling that none of them was ever good enough and that she wanted to possess me.

8. She didn't encourage me to succeed but instead criticized me constantly. I could never do anything right for her; nothing was ever good enough, no matter how hard I tried.

9. She seemed to have no understanding of what my problems were or of how I might feel in any given situation.

There were several times when I would be having a personal crisis and she would have no idea about it whatsoever. No matter how unhappy I was, she just didn't seem to notice.

Read your own list over several times, paying attention to how you feel each time you read it. It may make you feel angry, and it will probably bring up a lot of emotional pain. Allowing yourself to feel and express whatever emotions surface will help you come out of denial, face the truth about your childhood and your parents, and make your decision as to whether divorce is the healthy choice for you.

Read your list out loud to a trusted friend or loved one. If applicable, ask her if she remembers anything that you have forgotten to put on your list.

Since we sometimes forgive a little too readily what a parent has done to us, make a list of the things your parent has done to hurt other people. Rolando had been in a terrible conflict as to whether or not he should divorce his father. No matter what his father did to him, Rolando kept making excuses for his behavior. It wasn't until he wrote the following list that he was able to get it into his head how very abusive his father was.

1. My dad used to lock my little sister in the closet because she wouldn't stop crying.

2. Later on, he began to sexually abuse her. I was afraid of him, so I couldn't do anything about it.

3. As she became more and more withdrawn, he would make fun of her for being so shy. This made her even more shy and withdrawn.

4. I think he made her pregnant and then sent her away to a home for unwed mothers, where she stayed for nearly a year.

5. When she started rebelling by staying out late at night and coming home drunk, he would beat her mercilessly.

6. He became more and more critical of her as she got older,

and to this day he doesn't have a nice word to say about her.

7. When my sister discovered that she was an alcoholic and started to go to Alcoholics Anonymous, he refused to believe it and told her that those people were all nuts.

8. When her husband committed suicide, he said that it was her fault—that she had made his life so miserable that he had decided to kill himself rather than live with her.

Unfortunately, we often care more for others than we care for ourselves, and we become upset more easily over how our parents have treated someone we love than we do about how they have treated us. Sometimes we have to look at a situation through someone else's eyes before we can see it objectively. If it takes looking at what your parent did to others in order for you to get in touch with your anger and with the truth about your parent, then you must do whatever is necessary.

## SEPARATING THE PAST FROM THE PRESENT

Although the way your parent mistreated or neglected you as a child certainly affects the way you feel about her today, it is how she treats you today that is the most important factor in determining whether or not you will divorce her.

What exactly does your parent do now that is unacceptable to you? List all the ways that she continues to be abusive, controlling, manipulative, or neglectful.

Here is an excerpt from my own list:

1. My mother doesn't take an interest in the things that are important to me. She doesn't ask about my work or my relationship.

2. She tries to manipulate me with guilt.

3. She continues to try to tell me how to run my life.

4. She refuses to acknowledge how her behavior in the past still affects me in the present.

5. She constantly gives me double messages, saying one thing and then denying that she meant it when I confront her with it.

6. She continues to be extremely secretive and refuses to be honest about events of my childhood, about my father, and so on.

Many emotions will undoubtedly be stirred up when you write this list, and you may become keenly aware that you do not want to be around someone who treats you this way. Since these feelings will tend to fade as time passes and you begin once more to rationalize and minimize your parent's behavior, read over your list from time to time as a way of breaking through these defenses. Tell yourself that you do not deserve this kind of treatment and that you deserve to be treated with respect, consideration, and caring. Ask yourself what the chances are of your parent's changing and beginning to treat you in the ways that you want and deserve to be treated.

## RELEASING YOUR ANGER

In her book, *For Your Own Good*, about the hidden cruelty in much child rearing, Alice Miller writes:

The individual psychological stages in the lives of most people are:

1. To be hurt as a small child without anyone recognizing the situation as such.

2. To fail to react to the resulting suffering with anger.

3. To show gratitude for what are supposed to be good intentions.

4. To forget everything.

5. To discharge the stored-up anger onto others in adulthood or to direct it against oneself.

Before you decide to divorce one or both of your parents, it is important that you release your anger toward them. Otherwise, you will stay stuck in your childhood, unable to see your parents for who they are today. Many adult children have found that once they have released their repressed anger, they are able to see their parents in a more compassionate light.

Some adult children want to hold onto their anger, because they are afraid that if they release it they will become too vulnerable to their parents. They believe that as long as they remain enraged they will have the strength to stay away. But repressed anger actually does the opposite, weakening us and making us more vulnerable. Releasing your anger toward your parent can give you the courage to divorce him and strengthen your determination to not allow him to continue to ruin your life.

Most parents refuse to listen to their adult children's anger and, in fact, refuse to believe that they have a right to that anger. If parents would allow their adult children to express their anger toward them directly for all the ways they have abused or neglected them, divorcing a parent would be unnecessary. You may have tried to express your anger directly to your parent several times, only to have him defend himself, deny any responsibility, argue with you, manipulate you by appearing deeply hurt, or try to shut you up in some way.

Fortunately, you need not express your anger directly to your parents to benefit. In my book *The Right to Innocence: Healing the Trauma of Childhood Sexual Abuse*, I listed several excellent anger-releasing techniques, as follows:

### Physical Exercises

In all the physical releases, inhale deeply before making any sudden exertion, and remember to keep breathing. Let out a sound with each exhale whenever you can ; say the word *no* or some other word that expresses your anger. You might place a picture of the person with whom you are angry nearby when you do some of the physical releases.

HITTING

1. Purchase an "encounter bat" or "bataca" (a foam bat available in most sporting-goods stores), or use a plastic bat or old

tennis racquet. Place a large pillow before you on the floor, or position yourself on or next to your bed. Get on your knees, lift the bat directly over your head, and bring it down hard in a swift movement. You can envision the person you are angry with, but as you hit make sure your eyes are wide open and focused on a spot on the pillow or bed.

2. Punch a punching bag or punch the air, as in shadowboxing.

3. Pound pillows with your fists. Lie on your back on the floor or on your bed. Place pillows at your sides, directly beneath your hands.

4. Hit a piece of furniture with a rolled-up towel, newspaper, or magazine.

5. Play a sport that requires a hitting action, such as tennis, racquetball, or volleyball. Focus on releasing anger while you are hitting.

6. Punch clay, dough, or any other pliable material.

KICKING AND STOMPING

1. Stomp on old egg cartons or aluminum cans.

2. Kick a large pillow or ball.

3. Take a walk, and each time you take a step imagine that you are stomping on the person with whom you are angry.

4. Do karate kicks.

5. Do scissors kicks on a bed or mat.

PUSHING

1. Place two large pillows against a wall. Lie on your back. Using your feet and legs, kick and push the pillows as hard as you can against the wall. (This is especially effective for women who have been raped or violently assaulted.)

2. Facing a wall or door, stand with your arms straight out in front of you, an arm's length from the wall or door. With feet planted firmly on the floor, start pushing as hard as you can

against the wall. Say out loud, "Get away from me," or "Leave me alone."

### THROWING

1. Throw unwanted dishes, raw eggs, or water balloons against your garage wall, back fence, or garbage can.

2. Throw pillows against the wall. Make sure to let out a sound, saying something like "No!" or "Get away!" or "Take that!" as you do so.

3. Throw balls or darts.

4. Throw rocks into a river or into the ocean.

### TEARING

1. Tear an old phone book or newspapers into pieces.

2. Tear up old pillows, sheets, or rags.

### SCREAMING AND YELLING

1. Put your face into a pillow and scream as hard as you can.

2. Yell and scream in the shower.

3. Turn the TV or radio up loud and scream.

4. Scream and yell on amusement-park "thrill" rides.

5. Scream long and loud in a quiet, private place.

6. Roll up your car windows, turn your radio up loud, and scream as long and hard as you can.

---

### Writing Exercises

In the following exercises, write whatever comes to mind without censoring yourself. Remember that no one will ever need to see what you have written.

1. Write a letter to the person you are angry with, expressing exactly how you feel. This letter is intended for releasing

anger, not for mailing. Don't ask *questions* (such as "How could you . . .?" or "Why did you . . .?"), since questions help maintain your role as victim. Instead, make *statements*, using "I"—for example, "I'm angry with you for what you did . . . " or "I don't like what you did . . . " Be assertive. When you are done, you may either tear up the letter or keep it.

This is part of a letter I wrote to my mother (that I did not send) when I was deciding whether or not to divorce her:

> Mother, I hate you for what you have made me into—I hate you for hurting the little child in me so much that she will probably never be able to love freely without fearing rejection and criticism. I hate you because I have been so damaged by you—so messed up sexually, emotionally, and even spiritually. You not only robbed me of my childhood, my innocence, and my self-esteem, but you continue to rob me of a chance to love, a chance to be peaceful, a chance to be whole.
>
> I was a beautiful, loving, intelligent, and talented child, and you systematically set out to destroy me. You tried to destroy my beauty by stuffing me with unhealthy food, by dressing me like a ragamuffin, by not teaching me how to brush my teeth, and by filling me with hatred. You tried to take away the love inside of me by hating me, criticizing me, teaching me that I couldn't trust others, and teaching me that to love is to be foolish, that loving means getting hurt. You tried to destroy my intelligence by never encouraging me in school, by coming in and yelling at me for keeping the light on late at night while I studied, by making me doubt my perceptions, by making me think my ideas were stupid. And you tried to destroy my talent by telling me that no one makes a living as an artist or a writer, that no one would buy my first book.
>
> Well, you did a pretty good job of destroying me. It has taken me 41 years to repair the damage. But the little child is still inside me, as beautiful, loving, intelligent,

and talented as she ever was. And I am becoming more beautiful, loving, intelligent, and talented every day.

2. Complete the following sentences:
   I am angry at my mother because . . .
   I am angry at my father because . . .

### Fantasizing and Imagining Exercises

For some people, it may be easier to *imagine* releasing their anger rather than to release it through physical or written exercises.

1. Have an imaginary conversation with the person you are angry with. Tell that person exactly how you feel; don't hold anything back.

2. Pretend the person you are angry with is sitting in a chair across from you. It may help to put a picture of the person on the chair. Talk to the empty chair or the picture and tell that person off.

3. Express your feelings of anger by talking into a tape recorder, saying everything you have ever wanted to say as if you were talking directly to your parent.

## LISTENING TO YOUR INNER VOICE

There is a voice inside each of us that can be described as our inner voice or the voice of our "higher self." While this concept can sound mysterious, it really is not. Your inner voice is that voice deep inside that provides you with your clearest insights. It is the reflection of your most accurate self-knowledge. This voice speaks to you often, and you can hear it if you pay attention.

For example, think of the times when you have wanted dessert but were watching your weight. More than likely there was a voice inside you that said, "No, don't have the dessert." When and if you listen to this voice, you probably feel better about yourself. When you ignore this voice, you don't.

To better understand what your inner voice is, it may be helpful to know what it is not. It's not the part of the mind that engages in lengthy analysis or dialogue. Your inner voice is not your will; for your inner voice to be useful, you have to listen to it and use your will to act on the insights you hear. Neither is your inner voice the stream of emotions. Though the inner voice communicates through feelings, it is better understood as that part of the self where feelings and thinking meet.

There can also be other voices in our head. Often, clients confuse their inner voice with the voice of a parent. Through a process called "introjection" we internalized our parents' messages to us when we were children. As children, carrying our protective parents around within us was necessary in order for us to feel safe. Unfortunately, we sometimes internalize the parent's critical voice as well and carry it into adulthood. When we are adults, we hear this critical voice whenever we have done something we think is bad or wrong. If you hear a voice inside you whenever you succumb to temptation that says things like, "You shouldn't have eaten that dessert—when are you ever going to learn?" or "What a pig! Are you happy now that you've gained five pounds?" You are hearing a critical-parent voice.

Don't mistake this for your inner voice. Your higher self does not chastise you *after* the fact. It is there to tell you what you should do *before* you make a decision. It is on your side.

People from dysfunctional families are not accustomed to listening to their own true voice. If you are constantly thinking negative thoughts about yourself, if you are always beating yourself up, one or both of your parents were probably very critical of you. Try to catch yourself when you think a critical, negative thought about yourself, and try to discover where you got that message. Whose voice is it you are hearing—your own, or that of your parent?

While your higher self will not steer you wrong, your critical-parent voice may, since its purpose is not to guide you but to make you conform to rules and expectations set up by others. Your higher self is not concerned with rules and shoulds, but with what is best for you.

### Letting Your Inner Voice Guide You

The messages of your inner voice can help you to decide whether to divorce your parent. First, however, you must cultivate your ability to hear it. As long as your mind is engaged and occupied with all your daily concerns, you won't be able to hear the quiet messages from your deepest self.

The following exercise was partly taken from the book, *Inner Joy,* by Harold H. Bloomfield and Robert B. Kory. It will take approximately 10 minutes to do, and will help you to contact your inner voice. The more you practice it, the more you will understand it. After you have learned to make contact with your inner voice, you will no longer need to use the technique. You can pause for a moment anytime, anywhere, and tune in to the messages from your deepest self.

1. Make sure you are alone and in a quiet place where you will not be disturbed. Get into a comfortable position, preferably lying on your back. Close your eyes and take three or four deep breaths through your nose. Notice the soothing effects of the air filling your lungs, then flowing out through your nostrils.

2. Systematically relax all the muscles in your body. Start with your toes and slowly work your way up the body, first tensing the muscles and then relaxing them as much as possible. Relax your feet, calves, knees, thighs, hips, abdomen, buttocks, back, chest, shoulders, neck, hands, arms, and face. Allow the warm heaviness of relaxation to spread throughout your body.

3. Now imagine that you are floating in space or lying in a warm meadow. Create any mental image that you find peaceful and deliciously enjoyable. Let the world slip away and drift naturally into your reveries.

4. Once you have relaxed, with each exhalation of breath mentally repeat the word *one* or any other simple syllable to yourself.

5. After several minutes, when you are feeling at ease, begin to notice that you're able to sit back and observe the flow of thoughts and feelings in your mind and body.

6. To create a quite inner space, make a decision to set all your problems and daily concerns aside. You needn't try to force thoughts out of your mind; all that is really required is a decision to set them aside. The idea is not to forget your problems, but to put them in an orderly perspective (much like making a list of things you have to do). Once you have cleared this inner space, you will settle more deeply into yourself. You will begin to have a more intimate sense of your total bodily state. You may notice tension in a muscle or a worry nagging somewhere in the back of your mind. These subtle feelings indicate that you're clearing space to learn what's really going on inside.

7. Now focus on the problem at hand—in this case, whether or not you should divorce your parent. Be aware of the problem without focusing on it too closely and intensely. Notice any feelings that begin to emerge from within. You will probably encounter some intense emotions. Don't try to analyze your emotions, and don't try to push them away. Just allow yourself to notice and express them. As you allow repressed pain to surface, you'll feel a great sense of relief and emotional freedom. Let the feelings grow on their own. If a feeling shifts, follow it, but don't force it. Attend to it as if you were watching an interesting movie. Gradually, the feeling will take on a recognizable shape.

8. The last step is to put your feelings into words. The feeling will give you a new perspective on the problem, so don't hurry to label it with stock phrases. Take an experimental attitude. Words will come up. Gently match them against the feeling. If there's an approximate match, you'll have a deep, inner sense of rightness. There will be a click, perhaps an "Aha!" If the match is not good, the sense of rightness will be fuzzy. As you work with words to describe your feeling, use this sense of

rightness as your guide. It is very similar to the sense of rightness you have when you adjust a crooked picture. When the picture is straight, you simply feel that it's right. So, too, with finding the words to understand the new feeling from your inner voice: when it's clear, you'll feel it's right.

You may have to use this technique several times in order to get a clear answer to your question. You may feel ambivalent about the messages you hear or about a feeling you have. Ask yourself, "What does this feeling mean?" and wait for a response. If after 10 minutes you feel no click of understanding, no sense of rightness to anything that has come up, let it be. Come back later and do the exercise again. Be patient! The answer will come, and it will be the right answer for you.

Your inner voice may start out as just a soft whisper, but the more you listen to it and act on what it says, the stronger and clearer it will become.

## PHYSICAL AND EMOTIONAL CLUES

Whenever we are in conflict, our bodies and our emotions react strongly, often giving us important physical and emotional clues that can help us resolve the conflict. This is particularly true when we are around someone with whom we have strong negative or conflictual feelings.

Our bodies reflect our emotional state so your body can tell you a lot about what is good for you and what is not. Your body and your emotions, working together, can give you important clues about how you are feeling around your parent, and equally important, can help you to know how you feel when you are away from him.

How do you feel when you think of going to see one or both of your parents?

Do you look forward to seeing them?

Do you feel fearful or anxious about seeing them?

Do you become physically ill or extremely tired?

Do you become depressed?

Do you feel resentful at "having" to see them?

Do you look for excuses not to see them?

How do you feel after you have been with one or both your parents for a while?

Do you feel anxious, nervous, or afraid?

Do you feel on guard?

Do you feel angry?

Do you begin to feel trapped?

Do you start looking forward to going home?

How do you feel right after you have left them?

Are you relieved to be away from them?

Do you regret having seen them?

Do you feel better or worse about yourself?

What emotions do you feel?
Do you wish you hadn't gone?

Are you angry at yourself for going?

Do you feel guilty for having left when you did? Do you feel guilty for having wanted to leave or for wishing you hadn't come, or for not having liked being in your parents' presence?

What aftereffects do you feel from the visit?

Do you eat too much when you get home?

Do you feel compelled to have a drink or take drugs?

Do you snap at your mate or your children?

Are you overly critical of others? Of yourself?

Do you do something to try to sabotage any success you may have accomplished or any good relationship you may have?

Do you try to escape your feelings by sleeping, watching TV, or reading?

Do you feel despondent and have a hard time holding back the tears?

Do you become physically self-destructive (for example, by picking at your skin or jabbing yourself with sharp instruments)?

Do you feel hopeless and suicidal?

Do you drive recklessly or have fantasies of running your car into the center divider on the freeway?

How long does it generally take you to "recover" from your visits with your parents?

Do you fall into a deep depression for days or even weeks?

Do you go on a drinking, eating, shopping, gambling, or sex binge?

Do you and your mate argue for days, or do you remain distant from your mate and other loved ones for several days following a visit with your parents?

Do you have a difficult time at work or school for several days or weeks?

If many of these things happen to you after seeing one or both of your parents, your body and your emotions are trying to tell you that it is unhealthy for you to be around them right now. Listen to these important messages. While you may feel compelled to see them out of guilt or loneliness, the price you pay may be too great.

## BEFORE YOU DECIDE TO DIVORCE

Before you decide to divorce one or both of your parents, I would recommend that you do at least one of the following (1) seek professional help; (2) have a formal confrontation with your parent; or (3) try a temporary separation. All three suggestions are aimed at helping you to be absolutely certain that divorcing your parent is truly what you want and need to do. Each will provide you with valuable information about yourself, your feelings, and your parents.

### Seeking Professional Help

Although you should not allow anyone to pressure you into making such an important decision, this doesn't mean that you shouldn't seek professional help with your conflict. Therapy can be of tremendous benefit in helping you work through your individual concerns and conflicts regarding divorce, look more objectively at the pros and cons, and prepare you for making the break if you choose to do so.

But even a therapist should not be allowed to tell you what to do. Find a therapist who can be objective about the issue, one who doesn't have any preconceived ideas about divorcing parents. Unfortunately, some therapists have strong beliefs about families staying together at all costs or about the necessity of forgiving parents for whatever they have done.

One of the main questions to ask a potential therapist when interviewing her is what her personal beliefs are regarding forgiveness. If she believes that you should always work toward forgiveness, that this forgiveness will come from your understanding that your parents were probably abused or neglected themselves, and that your anger only hurts you, then this person may be too biased to work with. She may not be able to understand that sometimes there are acts that cannot be forgiven, that if someone does not admit that he has done wrong it is difficult to forgive him for it, or that even if we are able to forgive, it may not be possible to be around that person.

Here are some other important questions to ask a potential therapist:

1. Have you worked with adult children of abusive families?
2. Do you think that adult children have a right to be angry with parents who were abusive?
3. How do you work to help people release their anger? (The reason for this question is that some therapists are uncomfortable with anger and especially with clients who release anger during the sessions. You will need someone who is not afraid of anger and will encourage you to release yours; otherwise, he or she might push forgiveness.)
4. Do you think it is necessary to forgive parents in order to recover?
5. Do you think there are acts that can be unforgivable?
6. Do you think divorcing a parent can be a healthy choice? If so, under what circumstances?

Divorcing a parent is a difficult enough thing to do without having to deal with resistance from your therapist. Be sure you get one who is open-minded and can give you the support you so need and deserve.

### Confronting Your Parent

As I mentioned earlier, it is important that you try everything possible before deciding to divorce your parent. This includes having a formal confrontation with him in which you tell him exactly how he has hurt you and how you feel about him, what it is that he is doing now that is unacceptable to you, and what it is that you would like from him, including how you expect him to treat you.

If you are planning to divorce both parents, it is usually best to confront each one individually. You probably have separate issues with each, and you may feel "ganged up on" if you confront them both together.

Confronting your parent enables you to take back your power, proving to yourself that you are no longer going to allow him to frighten or control you. By facing your parent with the truth and with your feelings, no matter how frightened you are, you are breaking the cycle of victimization and are no longer being impotent, passive, and ineffectual, allowing things to happen to you.

Don't set yourself up with false hopes and fantasies that your parent will suddenly see the error of his ways and will apologize profusely. Expect him to deny, claim to have forgotten, project the blame back onto you, and get very angry. But no matter how the confrontation turns out, consider it successful simply because you have had the courage to do it. This confrontation symbolizes the beginning of change in the balance of power between you and your parent.

It can be extremely frightening to experience your parents' anger. They may become insulting, bitter, or threatening when you stand up to them and tell them you are going to run your life *your* way. It can be painful to see their pain and disappointment when you tell them no—no, you aren't going to do as they suggest; no, you aren't coming over now; no, you aren't going to become what they wanted you to become. You may be afraid they will say, "In that case, to hell with you" in response to your show of autonomy.

But what have you got to lose? If your parents are going to reject you for standing up for yourself, the price is far too high. If you have to choose between them or yourself, you have to choose yourself.

Perhaps you have had one or more confrontations with your parents already. While I certainly wouldn't blame you for not wanting to try again, maybe this time you are in a different place, or maybe they are. At any rate, it is worth a try.

Practice your confrontation by writing it down, speaking into a tape recorder, or just talking out loud. You can practice by yourself, with a friend, or with a therapist. The following suggested format can be used as a guide or script.

1. List what your parent did to make you feel angry, hurt, damaged, guilty, ashamed, or afraid. State each abuse, injustice, injury, damage, and painful memory you have.
   Examples:
   You neglected me terribly when I was a child.
   You robbed me of my innocence and betrayed my trust by sexually molesting me.
   You didn't protect me.
   You beat me mercilessly and locked me in the closet.

2. List how you felt as a result of your parent's behavior toward you.
   Examples:
   I felt unloved and unworthy of being loved.
   I felt so dirty and ugly inside.
   I felt so ashamed.
   I felt frightened and alone.
   I felt angry but afraid to show you my anger.

3. List what effects your parent's behavior has had on you, both during your childhood and in your adult life.
   Examples:
   *As a child:*
   It affected my ability to trust.
   It caused me to live in fear.
   It caused me to have very low self-esteem.
   It caused me to be a bully to others.
   *As an adult:*
   It has caused me to be self-destructive.
   It has destroyed my feelings of self-worth.
   It has affected my sexuality and my health.

4. Tell your parent how you feel about him *now*, and why.
   Examples:
   I feel angry with you for damaging my life.
   I feel afraid you will let me down again.
   I am afraid you will molest my children.

5. List everything you want from him *now*.
   Examples:
   I want you to listen to me and believe me.

I want you to get help.

I want you to stay away from my children.

Before you confront your parent, you will need to make the following preparations:

1. Take the edge off your anger by using any of the anger-releasing techniques listed earlier in this chapter.

2. Rehearse your confrontation until you are sure of what you want to say.

3. Decide when and where you would like to have the confrontation. Where would you feel most comfortable, secure, and confident? Some people prefer their own turf; others prefer a neutral place. Some choose to meet in a public place such as a park so they can get away quickly if they need to. Many prefer to have the confrontation take place in their therapist's office. If you are apprehensive about violence or loss of control, you may need to have a third party present—even if it is your *own* rage or loss of control that you fear.

4. Set some ground rules for the confrontation, and determine how you will express these to your parent. Here are some examples:

   I want you to hear me out before you respond.

   I don't want you to interrupt me or stop me.

   I don't want you to defend, justify, or rationalize.

5. Obtain a commitment to the ground rules from your parent *before* you proceed. If your parent is unwilling to do even this much, it is probably better to try the confrontation at a later date. Remember, you have the advantage. You are prepared and you have decided when, where, and under what circumstances the confrontation will take place.

6. Even if your parent does agree to your ground rules, be prepared for a counterattack both during and after your

confrontation. Expect the worst, including any of the following responses:

*Denial* ("You're lying," "You're exaggerating," "I don't remember," or "That never happened.")

*Blame* ("You were such a difficult child," "You're crazy," "I had to do something to control you.")

*Rationalizations* ("I did the best I could," "Things were really tough," "I tried to stop drinking but I couldn't.")

*Self-pity* ("I have enough problems without this," "How could you do this to me?")

*Guilt* ("Look what we did for you," "Nothing was ever enough for you," "This is the thanks I get!")

7. Make sure you have supportive people to talk to before and after your confrontation.

8. Be prepared to end the confrontation whenever you decide its effectiveness is over, if you feel threatened or fear you are losing control, if your parent is too busy defending himself to really hear you, or if the confrontation has turned into a shouting match.

No matter how clear, reasonable, or articulate you are in your confrontation or in your responses to your parent's counterattacks, your parent may twist your words and your motives, accuse, lie, and make you feel as if you are crazy. Keep in mind, however, that confrontations that end in anger can sometimes lead to positive changes once the initial uproar is over. Give your parent some time to think about what you have said before you assume that she didn't hear you or didn't take what you said seriously.

If your parent has shown some capacity for understanding your pain and some willingness to take responsibility for her actions, however small this capacity may seem, there may be hope for the relationship. If she is willing to continue discussing the conflicts between the two of you, you may be able to teach her what does and what doesn't feel good to you in the relationship.

Unlike ventilating anger, confronting is most effective when done face-to-face. Unfortunately, this is not always possible. It may be too dangerous if there is a risk of being reabused. Or, your parent may be medically or psychologically fragile and thus incapable of withstanding a direct confrontation.

If a face-to-face confrontation is not possible or is too threatening there are other ways to confront. Using the format above, you can write a confrontation letter or make a tape of your confrontation on a tape recorder.

Sometimes it is our parents who do the divorcing when we finally stand up to them and confront them about their behavior, expose a family secret, or start to break away. Even though you may not be the one who initiates the divorce, make sure that you come from a position of choice and allow the divorce to proceed. For example, if your parent rejects you for standing up for yourself, then you have a choice to *let it be* and not get hooked back into trying to reason with him, please him, or placate him. Don't let him threaten you into submission one more time, especially since you have been considering divorcing him in the first place.

You knew the risks when you first decided to confront your parent with the truth. Remind yourself that you decided to confront because you couldn't tolerate the ways things were. If your parent cannot tolerate hearing the truth or cannot deal with who you now are, then the healthy thing would have been for you to stop seeing him anyway.

Marshall's mother started being sexually seductive toward him when he began to enter puberty. She would walk around the house with little or nothing on and act "surprised" when he saw her. She would also "mistakenly" walk in on him while he was showering, using the toilet, or dressing. When he began to lock the door to the bathroom, she acted hurt and insulted. She would ask him to give her a massage because her back hurt, and she would offer to rub his sore muscles if he complained after playing baseball. She tried to engage him in conversation about girls he might be attracted to or about the sexual relationship she had had with his father before he died.

Marshall was constantly embarrassed by his mother's advances, but at the same time he sometimes felt aroused. When this happened he was mortified. "I can't tell you how utterly ashamed I was over these feelings," he said. "I would feel like the scum of the earth for being turned on to my own mother! Now, of course, I realize I was only responding like a normal boy to sexual stimuli, but then I couldn't understand how I could feel like that."

Because of his mother's continual seductiveness, Marshall had a love/hate relationship with her. He loved her because in every other way she was very kind to him, and he appreciated the fact that she'd been supporting them since his father's death. He took the fact that his mother never dated as a sign of her loyalty to him and to his father, and he felt proud of her because she wasn't like so many of the other single mothers he knew who went out drinking and picking up men. But he hated her for being sexual with him and putting him in such a bind. He had to refuse her advances, and yet he became increasingly aroused while in her presence.

Marshall's mother continued her seductive behavior even after he became an adult. Wearing low-cut blouses and tight pants, she would come up to him and put her arms around him.

> I would feel like I was going to be smothered, she held me so close. I tried to avoid having anything to do with her physically, but she made that impossible. She'd grab me before I could get away. For years, I just couldn't bring myself to tell her to stop because I knew her feelings would be terribly hurt. but finally I realized that I had to confront her and tell her to stop. I had nothing to lose at that point, because if I didn't tell her I would have to stop seeing her. Well, I told her, and she became enraged. She accused me of having been attracted to *her* all those years, and she claimed that she had just been putting up with it all that time not to hurt my feelings. She said that she was extremely humiliated that I would accuse her of such a thing. At that point I realized I had to break all ties with her.

It had been unhealthy for Marshall to be around his mother because of her seductiveness with him, but now it was even more unhealthy because she refused to tell the truth and had turned things around in order to save face. Continuing the relationship with her under these circumstances would have left Marshall in an abusive situation; fortunately, he realized this.

## Testing the Waters: The Temporary Separation

It may be important for you to temporarily separate from your parent so that you can test out some of your fears—for example, the fear that you will not survive without a parent. Often such a fear is left over from childhood, when we needed our parents in order to survive. By temporarily separating from your parent, you can prove to yourself that the adult you are now certainly can survive and can also take care of the child within.

A temporary separation can be an excellent alternative to an out-and-out divorce if you are wracked with conflict about taking that final step. Many people view the temporary separation as more of a trial separation, a time to test how they feel about not seeing their parents. They may still want to give their parents a chance to treat them differently. And—although this should *not* be your primary purpose for a temporary separation—one of the benefits can be that it gives your parents time to think things over as well. Some parents have indeed missed their adult children enough to be willing to make some changes. Lupe, a client of mine who had separated from her mother for six months, found that her mother missed her so much she agreed to go into therapy with her in order to work on their problems.

While you are still seeing your parent, you may both stay locked in the same negative patterns of communication and behavior. Time away from each other may help you to distance yourself enough that you do not get "hooked" back into these negative patterns. It may also help you to be more objective about your parent. With more emotional distance, you and your parent might rediscover some genuine positive feelings for each other.

On the other hand, the objectivity about your parents that you gain from a temporary separation may help you decide not to continue the relationship with them, as was the case with Marjorie. Although Marjorie chose to separate from her parents temporarily in order to get a better perspective, the separation became a permanent one:

> When you are in the midst of something, it's hard to see the truth about it. If you grow up with a lie, you have to step back from it or you can't see the forest for the trees. I had to break away from my family in order to discover who they really are. There were so many lies in my family and my parents had so many masks and facades that it was hard to know who they really were or what was really going on. This was particularly true of my perception of my mother. Breaking away from her enabled me to see her for who she really is and to see elements of the relationship that I had been blinded to. If it hadn't been for these breaks I would have continued to believe her—believe that she really cared about me when she clearly doesn't, believe the false front she puts on for everyone.
>
> Because I stayed away from my entire family for a while, I was also able to see my sisters more clearly as well. I now realize that one of them is just like my mother, pretending to care, giving lip service to caring, but all the while being incapable of truly understanding how I feel or of standing up for me against my dad. With some time away, I have been able to see my other sister more clearly also and I was pleasantly surprised at what I saw. I always felt abused by her, since she was so critical and distant. But she has really been the only one to stand by me. She has attended several therapy sessions with me, and my therapist and I in turn have gone with her to see *her* therapist. We have helped each other to fill in the blank spots in our childhood memories.
>
> I've also learned a lot by observing how my family responded when I separated from them. Instead of acting concerned about the fact that I didn't want to see her for a while, much to my surprise my mother seemed to actually be relieved not to have to deal with me anymore. I realized what a burden it had been for her to have to continually put up the facade of being a caring mother. I gave her the perfect out, and she took it. I had fully intended to divorce my father, but I really thought I would eventually reconcile with my mother. My temporary separation from her has turned into a permanent one.

A trial separation can be very painful, but it can also be a time of enormous growth. Since you will not be spending large amounts of time and energy on your conflicts with your parents, you will have more energy available for your own life and your recovery.

There is no recommended amount of time necessary for you to spend away from your parent. Some people find a brief period—of a few months—sufficient, while others have stayed away for years. Sometimes a temporary separation can evolve into a permanent one because it feels so good to get away that you wouldn't think of trying again. At other times it turns out that while the adult child may intend the separation to be only temporary, circumstances cause it to be a permanent split. When Carrie told her father she wasn't going to see him or talk to him while she was in recovery, he got so angry with her he told her that as far as he was concerned he no longer had a daughter.

Set up your time away in any way that feels right to you. You may choose to have a complete break with no communication at all, or you may want to simply limit the time you spend with your parent. Or, you might decide to communicate only by mail or by phone during your temporary separation. This is what Adena did. "I got so I just couldn't see my mother in person because I'd feel too trapped, but I could talk to her on the phone just to check in. Then, as soon as I got uncomfortable, I could say, 'I have to go.'"

You may choose to see your parent only at important functions, such as weddings, funerals, and anniversaries. Or you may limit your contact even further, sharing important news via letters and phone calls.

You will also need to decide how you will communicate to your parent your need for time away. You can do this in person, by mail, or by phone, telling your parent exactly why you don't wish to see him for a while. Holly told her father the truth: "I love you, but I can't be around you right now. Seeing you gets in the way of my recovery. I'll call you when I feel stronger." Many people aren't ready to be quite that honest. Instead, they just avoid their parents for a while, making up excuses as to why they can't see them.

If you do tell your parent about your intention to temporarily separate, make sure you are firm about your need for a break. Your parent may not take no for an answer and may insist on continuing to see you; she may even try to contact you more often than she did before. Remind yourself and your parent that if she really cares about you, she will respect your need for some time away.

While your parent may press you to tell her how long the separation will be, you probably will not know ahead of time. Some people feel that a temporary separation should be at least three months long. After this time you can reevaluate how you feel and extend the separation, resume the relationship, or make the separation permanent. As part of your evaluation you may wish to meet with your parent and see if she has changed at all. Or, you may base your decision about what to do next solely on how *you* have changed during the separation.

At this point, you have made a decision. As I am sure you have heard before, *not* deciding is also a decision. You have decided that you definitely do not wish to divorce your parent, that you are not yet ready to do so, that you wish to try a temporary separation, or that you are going to proceed with a divorce. This decision is based on what you feel right now, and it may change at any time. If you do not feel ready to divorce your parent at this time, for whatever reason, that is okay.

For many of you reading this book, it will be just a matter of time before you divorce your parent. At this point, however, you may still have some hope that the relationship can be salvaged. It is difficult to know when the time has come to give up hoping. Each of us must come to this major decision on our own, in our own time. Some people continue trying and hoping for years, while others feel they have already waited long enough. The main question you must ask yourself is this: "Do I see any signs, however small, of some *consistent* progress on the part of my parent?" Keep in mind how long it has taken you to be able to make your own changes. Don't expect an immediate positive response from your parent just because you are responding to *her* in a healthier way. And don't expect any initial changes in your parent to be major ones. Instead, look for small changes at first, such as less defensiveness on your parent's part when you want to talk about your childhood.

On the other hand, the price of continuing your relationship with your parent may simply be too high. Even though you may note some slight changes, her overall behavior and attitude toward you may still be too damaging and threatening for you to withstand.

You will know if and when you are ready to sever the ties. While it is important to try everything possible and view divorce only as a last resort, it serves no purpose to continue trying when nothing is being accomplished. If you've tried telling your parent the truth, only to have him deny it; if you've tried expressing your anger and working things out, only to have your parent turn on you and abuse you further; or if your parent continually "accuses and confuses" you, it may be time to stop trying. If your attempts to communicate or reconcile with your parent have fallen on deaf ears, it's probably time to stop talking.

There may come a time when you have to say, "No matter what is going on with my parent, I have to lead my own life. I can feel tenderness or empathy for my parent, but it doesn't mean I have to be around him or have a relationship with him. I can feel anger, but it doesn't mean I have to retaliate. I have to cut the cord for good."

# CHAPTER 4

# Preparing Yourself for Divorce

You are ready to divorce your parent when you have gained the inner knowledge that it is time to cease trying to resolve your conflicts with your parent, when you are not willing to continue the relationship as it is, and when you wish to make this known to your parent.

But saying good-bye to your parent is something you need to do internally long before you actually tell your parent about it or act on it. Even though you have made the decision to divorce your parent, there are still some preparatory tasks you will need to accomplish before going through with the divorce.

## PREPARING YOUR INNER CHILD

Even though you may have decided to divorce your parent, there is a part of you that will never think it is a good idea. That part of you is your inner child. Although you may not remember your early childhood feelings, we have all unknowingly incorporated into ourselves the child each of us once was, with a child's fears, insecurities, and desperate need to be loved. That child is as alive and with you and as forceful a presence as if he or she were living in your household.

When you are afraid to try, it is the child in you who is afraid to try. When you feel that you have to be good all the time to be loved, it is the little child within you who feels this way, who is still looking for what you wanted so desperately when you were little.

As surely as you would have to prepare a real child for a major change in her life (for example, starting school for the first time or moving to a new town), you will need to prepare your inner child for the loss of your parent. While you may be ready to divorce your parent, your inner child most assuredly is not. As noted in the last chapter, you—that is, your inner child—may fear that you will not survive without your parent, much as children cannot survive without their parents to provide for them and protect them.

## Discovering the Child Within

In order to prepare your inner child for the divorce, you must first connect with that child and become aware of how he or she feels. The following exercise will help you to contact your inner child.

1. Sit or lie down comfortably with your eyes closed.

2. Close your eyes and begin doing deep breathing, inhaling as much air as possible and then making sure to expel it all before you take another deep breath. Do this for a minute or two, or until you feel relaxed.

3. With your eyes still closed, visualize your inner child as you imagine she would look.

4. Notice how you feel about her. Do you like her?

5. Notice how she seems to feel about you. Does she seem open to you, or does she seem rejecting?

6. Try to make some contact with her, whether it be reaching out to touch her hand or hug her or just making eye contact with her. How does she react? Does she welcome contact with you, or does she turn away?

If you were able to visualize your inner child and then make positive contact with her on the first try, you are fortunate indeed. Many people are not able to visualize their inner child very easily the first time, and even those who do are often unable to have a positive connection with her.

My first experience with this exercise was typical. When I first tried to visualize my inner child, I just drew a blank. I couldn't see anything, no matter how hard I tried. After several tries I was finally able to visualize my inner child, but I found I didn't even like her! She was dressed in dirty clothes, her hair needed washing and combing, and her teeth even needed to be brushed. When I was asked to try to make contact with her, I didn't want to because she was so dirty. I realized that she looked the way I often had as a child. No wonder people outside my home hadn't been too eager to pay attention to me. I realized I would mentally have to give my inner child a bath, wash and comb her hair, and put clean clothes on her before I could be comfortable around her. Then, reluctantly, I held her on my lap. She wasn't too fond of me at first, either. But as I took care of her by cleaning her up, dressing her in a pretty dress, and putting bows in her hair, she finally warmed up to me, too.

If you are having a difficult time visualizing your inner child, try the following exercise:

1. Look through old family albums to find some pictures of yourself when you were a child. If they are available, pick out pictures of yourself as an infant, as a toddler, as a young child, and as an adolescent. Choose pictures that most remind you of how you felt at these particular ages.

2. After studying these pictures carefully, one by one, see if you can retain their images when you close your eyes. It might help to do the following:

Study your infant picture for several minutes.

Now, close your eyes and see if you can hold on to that image in your mind's eye.

If you cannot do so, try again. Continue until you can see
the image of yourself as an infant, a toddler, a young child,
and an adolescent at will.

This exercise should help you to do the visualization exercise
above. Try it again now, using the memories of the photos as
reminders of how you looked. You may choose different images at
different times, one day seeing the infant, another day the adolescent, and so on.

Once you have identified your inner child you can begin to
communicate with her, reassuring her that you are there for her
and finding out how she feels and what she needs. This can be
done through a verbal or written dialogue, an imaginary conversation between the adult part of you and the child part of you. Start
your dialogue with a question such as "How are you today?" or
"What's the matter? You seem upset—is something bothering
you?" As you practice this dialogue, your inner child will eventually be able to express what she is feeling. The adult part of you
will then be able to listen to the child, soothe her, and assume
responsibility for her, in essence becoming the good parent you
never had.

Many discover that their inner child is reluctant to trust them.
This was Paula's experience:

> I tried to hug my inner child, but she pushed me away. I asked her
> what was wrong, and she said she didn't want me to hold her be-
> cause she knew I didn't really love her. I told her I did love her, and
> she called me a liar. When I asked her why she thought that, she
> told me I've been ignoring her for so long! Well, she was right. I
> have been ignoring her and her needs for a long, long time. I told
> her I was sorry, and then I promised that I would work on paying
> attention to her needs more. At first she didn't believe me, but as
> time passed and she realized that I really was there for her, she
> began trusting me.

Your inner child needs to learn to trust that *you* (the adult part
of you) will protect and nurture her, not be neglectful and abusive

like the other adults in her life have been. Unfortunately, we often end up being as neglectful and abusive of our inner child as our parents were of us when we were children. We ignore our inner child, we are ashamed of her, and do not take care of her in appropriate ways. We pretend that her feelings of fear and insecurity and her need to be loved do not exist. We starve her emotionally, never giving her the soothing and comforting she needs.

In time, you can establish a good relationship wtih your inner child. You will need to continually work on connecting with her, asking her how she feels and what she needs from you. You will be surprised at how real her voice will become and at how much you will grow to depend on her to tell you what is going on with you.

### Reassuring Your Inner Child

Perhaps the strongest reason we have for maintaining a relationship with our parents, however destructive that relationship may be, is our intense fear that we will be all alone in a cold world. Even though you may be surrounded by a loving and caring spouse, children of your own, friends, and a support group or therapist, the child inside you may strongly resist "cutting the cord." Since the child inside does not know that he will survive if he does not have his parents, he will feel totally abandoned, helpless, and alone.

Therefore, it will be absolutely necessary for you to reassure him that he will not be alone at all but will have *you* (the adult part of you) to take care of him. The adult side of you is the part that makes you go to work even when you don't feel like it and take care of your children even when you are tired. This is the part of you that must now be there for your inner child while he goes through the trauma of losing his mother or father.

The adult part of you will also be mourning the loss of your parent, but it is far easier to deal with adult mourning than with a child's feelings of helplessness and abandonment. We will cover adult mourning in later chapters, *after you have already divorced your parent.* At this point, we need to focus on your inner child's anticipated feelings of loss. Your inner child is so panicky at the thought of losing a parent that he will do anything to hold onto that parent. After all, you are asking him to give up his mommy or daddy, and what child would willingly do this?

For this reason the child within may be at odds with the adult part of you and may end up controlling the adult if you aren't careful. The adult side of you will need to take charge of divorcing your parent and not allow the child to talk you into staying.

The only way your inner child will go along with your plan to divorce your parent is if he has implicit trust in your adult self to take care of him. He will feel so lost without his parent that he may make you weaken and run back to Mommy or Daddy. No matter how unavailable or abusive your parent really is, your inner child may force you to return time and time again. He would rather have the fantasy that there is still hope than face the fact that there is none. To your inner child, any mommy or daddy—no matter how abusive or neglectful—is better than no mommy or daddy at all. If he is going to allow you to take his mommy away, you'd better be sure to replace her with another parent first.

Although you may have people in your life now who can be supportive and caring, you cannot depend on anyone else to meet your child's needs. The adult that you are can provide the love and support your inner child so desperately needs and can act exactly as a good parent would act toward a cherished child.

### "Talking Turkey" to Your Inner Child

Another important part of preparing your inner child for the loss of your parent is to tell her about your intention to divorce before you do it, just as you would tell a real child. You can do this through a dialogue or in a letter. The following is a dialogue I had with my inner child:

CHILD: "I want to go see my mommy—I miss her!"

ADULT: "I know you do, honey, but we aren't going to see her anymore."

CHILD: "Why not? I love her!"

ADULT: "I know you do, but I have decided that it isn't good for us to see her."

CHILD: "Why?"

ADULT: "Because she isn't nice to us, and she makes us feel bad about ourselves."

CHILD: "She's nice to us sometimes."

ADULT: "Yes, but she is so changeable that I can't trust her."

CHILD: "She does say mean things sometimes, and it hurts my feelings."

ADULT: "Yes, she does, and that is why I am not going to expose you to that kind of hurt from her ever again."

CHILD: "But what will I do without my mommy? Who will take care of me?"

ADULT: "I am your mommy now. I will be a good mommy to you. I will take care of you."

CHILD: How will you take care of me? Will you play with me?"

ADULT: "I will take care of you by holding you when you cry, by listening to you when you are troubled, by making sure you get the proper food and rest, and by keeping you away from people who are abusive. And, yes, I will play with you."

CHILD: "You are going to do all that for me?"

ADULT: "Yes, and more."

CHILD: "Well, maybe it won't be so bad not seeing Mommy."

ADULT: "Maybe not. And if it is, I'll hold you while you cry.

And this is a letter my client Emily wrote to her inner child:

Dear Inner Child:
    First of all, I want you to know that I love you very much. I also want you to know that I am working very hard on being a good mommy to you, the kind of

mommy you need. I know that I have not always been a good mommy to you, and I know I have ignored many of your needs, but things are going to be different from now on. Next, I want you to know that I am going to get a divorce from my mother, and I plan on never seeing her again. I know this will scare you and make you very sad, but it isn't as if you are going to be alone. After all, you'll always have me. I know you are going to miss her, and so will I, but from now on it is just going to be you and me, and that's going to be enough.

Love,
Mommy

Although this dialogue and letter may sound somewhat corny or hokey to you, when you make a deep connection with your inner child you will relate to her in an entirely different way than you did at first. Dialogues and letters such as these touch a very deep and real part of us, a part that must be prepared if our efforts to sever ties with our parents are to be successful.

Gradually, you will come to realize that all the work you are doing with your inner child is actually preparation for the growth of the adult part of you. While the child has to be acknowledged, understood, and handled, it is the adult, after all, who is to do all the handling. And the adult in you will not only be taking care of the child but will also be in charge of directing your life from now on. In the beginning, your adult self may be weak and so may have difficulty giving support, love, and understanding to your inner child. But as the adult grows in her understanding, confidence, and handling of reality, and as she matures in the process, she will be more helpful to the child.

Just as a new parent begins to feel more and more confident as she realizes she is doing a good job with her new baby, we adults who are unskilled and untrained and who feel too immature to care for our inner child will gain courage, strength, and confidence as we reach out to that child and take good care of her. This is how our weak adult grows into a responsible parent. Through practice, through trial and error, through experiencing success, we are encouraged to do more of the same.

## AN EMOTIONAL DRESS REHEARSAL

In addition to preparing your inner child, you will need to practice saying good-bye to your parent. This will give you the courage to do it for real and will prepare you for the feelings that ending the relationship will evoke. You can do this practicing or role playing by yourself, with your therapist, in your support group, or with a friend. You can also practice saying good-bye by talking into a tape recorder or writing a letter that you do not send. Here are some exercises that many of my clients have found helpful:

1. Practice saying out loud to a trusted friend or loved one exactly what you would like to say to your parent as a way of saying good-bye. Ask your friend to remain silent, giving no feedback. Do this several times until you end up sounding the way you want to.

2. Do the same thing, but this time with your friend playing the role of your parent, responding to what you say in a way she might imagine your parent would. You may want to coach her beforehand, telling her about your parent and the way she normally responds to you. This will help your friend stay in character. After the exercise, ask your friend for feedback as to how you sounded and how she imagines your parent might feel about what you said.

3. Talk to an empty chair, imagining that it is your parent. When you have said everything you want to say, get up and sit in that chair. Now, play the role of your parent and respond the way you imagine he might respond to what you have just said. Change chairs and roles as often as you need to.

4. Practice saying good-bye to a picture of your parent.

5. Have a fantasy confrontation with your parent by doing the following:

     Lie down on your bed or couch and get as comfortable as possible. Close your eyes and begin to do deep breathing. Imagine that you are going to meet with your parent for the last time. Decide where this meeting will be. Try to choose a place where you will feel relatively safe (perhaps your home, a public place, or somewhere outdoors). Take a look around and notice the details of your meeting place (for example, the landscape or the furniture).

You are going to be in the unique position of being able to see your parent approach but he will not be able to see you. Notice how your parent looks—his posture, the expression on his face. Now, notice these same things as he spots you.

Sit down together. Tell your parent everything you have always wanted to say, since this will be the last time you will see each other. He will not be able to interrupt you or to respond until you are completely finished.

When you have said all that you want to say, imagine what your parent's response might be to what you have said.

Notice how your parent's comments have affected you. Now respond to his comments, standing up for yourself the best you can.

Once again, imagine how your parent would respond.

Now it is your turn again to defend yourself. You have the last word, so be sure you say everything you want to say. After you have finished, say good-bye. Say it several times quietly to yourself, and then say it out loud. Repeat it over and over, saying it louder as you go along.

Watch as your parent walks away. Notice how you are feeling.

These exercises can prepare you for the real thing. As you complete the exercises, notice how you are feeling. Are you feeling stronger now that you have proved to yourself you can say good-bye? Or are you feeling very frightened, realizing that you are not yet ready to say good-bye? If you're feeling afraid to say good-bye, write down all the reasons for your fears. This will help you to look at them more rationally.

If you found that you could not say good-bye, what is standing in your way? There are good reasons why you are not ready to do so at this time. Honor those feelings and write about them. Then try this exercise at another time.

## YOUR SUPPORTING CAST

Adult children who decide to divorce a parent will need a tremendous amount of support from friends and family. During this "scary limbo between the familiar and the new" (as Howard Halpern, author of *Cutting Loose*, calls it), your therapist, the members of your support group, and your friends and other loved ones will be vitally important in helping you through this difficult time.

Unfortunately, as I mentioned earlier, friends and family often do not agree with the decision to divorce a parent, so their support may not be forthcoming. In this case, you may need to develop a new support system and adopt a new "family."

For some people, a therapist has become the new parent, fulfilling many of their unmet needs for approval and undivided attention. For others, a Twelve-Step program, their sponsors, and the other people they meet in the program become their new family, providing structure, guidance, support, and acceptance. Some people are fortunate enough to have a mate who is very supportive and who offers a shoulder to cry on and open arms to comfort.

But many people do not have any of these supports. If you have no established support system, begin by making new friends—people who are understanding and who can give you the emotional support you need as you go through this important transition in your life. More and more people are aware of the devastation that coming from a dysfunctional family can cause in an adult's life, and these people will not judge you as harshly as others may have in the past. Joining a Twelve-Step group (such as Adult Children of Alcoholics, Al-Anon, or CODA [Codependents Anonymous]), or a group for incest survivors will help you to meet supportive people who have been through the same thing as you and who really understand.

In addition to joining already existing groups, you might decide to form a group specifically for people who are thinking about divorcing a parent or who have already done so. This book can serve as your guide. You can put a notice in your local newspaper or spread the word at your Twelve-Step or other group meetings. There are many people who feel just as alone as you do and who will be grateful for your interest in them.

It is very important that you do not isolate yourself from other people for too long a time. It is, of course, understandable that you may be afraid to reach out to others. After all, your wounds are fresh, and you don't want to be hurt again by opening up to other people. But throughout the divorce process you will need the support of others in order to maintain the courage to stand by your decision. And the more needs you have met by caring, supportive friends, the less likely you will be to pine away for your parent or return to the empty well one more time.

You may discover that you have a lot to overcome when it comes to reaching out to make new friends. Because you were abused, neglected, or betrayed by your parent, you probably have a difficult time trusting others. You may assume that others will betray you, mistreat you, or use you, as your parent did. In addition, you probably received such messages from your parents as "Don't trust other people," "Don't tell others your business," and "No one cares for you like your family." These messages may have damaged your ability to open up and confide in others, to ask for help, or to trust others. You may see your peers as threats and competition rather than as potential supporters.

As difficult as it may be, try to let down your defenses a little and allow new people into your life. Look for new role models, and work toward adopting a new family who can provide you with the love, caring, support, and respect you so need and deserve.

As important as it is to develop a support system, it is equally important that it be *healthy* support. Healthy support is when others listen to us, allow us the time and space to express our emotions, and encourage us to do what is best for us. Unhealthy support is when others tell us what to do and take care of us to the point at which we don't have to take care of ourselves. Be sure that you are surrounding yourself with people who know how to give healthy support.

Some people run right out and try to find a surrogate parent (other than a therapist) to replace the one they are in the process of divorcing. Many adult children have a tendency to become attracted to or befriend "parental" types of people who take on the role of the caretaker. This is especially true of those who do not have a romantic partner. Be careful not to fall into this trap. While the parent "stand-in" may appear to be very loving and caring, chances are that you will be attracted to the very same kind of person that your parent is. Keep in mind how hard you've worked to disconnect from your parent. Why would you want to get another one just like him? Try to differentiate between unhealthy attractions—those intense feelings of instant merging with someone—and attractions based on mutual caring, interests, and healthy needs.

The stage is set. Your inner child is prepared for the divorce, your adult is prepared to take care of your inner child, you've rehearsed your lines, and you have your supporting cast. The next part of the book will guide you through the divorce itself and help you deal with its impact on your life.

# PART two

# Making the Divorce Final

# CHAPTER 5

# Coping with External and Internal Critics

Having made the decision to divorce your parent is only half the battle. The other half is in sticking to your decision once the pressure is on. You will be under a lot of pressure from others to explain why you have decided to divorce your parent, and you'll be criticized, misjudged, and misunderstood for doing so. In addition, periodically you'll feel guilty and doubt whether you have made the right decision.

## HOW TO HANDLE PRESSURE FROM OTHERS

Don't expect to be supported or understood by others when you divorce a parent. Few people can understand why you have gone to this extreme, even after you have explained it to them. You may be confronted with such questions as "Why can't you just let bygones by bygones?" or "Your parents are old—can't you just be more patient with them?" or "Your parents are too old to change—why can't you just accept them for who they are?" Such questions can make you feel misunderstood and criticized by the very people from whom you most need support.

Friends and loved ones, however well-meaning, almost always

discourage adult children from divorcing their parents. They do not understand, and instead of listening so they can understand, they may try to do all the talking, giving advice based on their own needs and experience. Their advice may be coming from their desire to protect either you or your parent from what they see as needless pain. However, it may only serve to confuse you further, making you feel selfish and bad for having the feelings you do and causing you to feel even more isolated and different.

## Dispelling the Myths

A person who decides to divorce a spouse often gets lots of support from friends and family. Not so in the case of adult children. There is no permission given in our society to honor our feelings regarding divorcing a parent. In fact, we are inundated with messages to the contrary. You may have already heard some of the "wisdom" I have listed below, and you will undoubtedly hear a lot more. These statements can confuse you, make you feel guilty and selfish, and ultimately cause you to doubt yourself and your decision. For this reason, I have countered the well-meaning advice of each statement that follows by dispelling the myth on which it is based. With this information, you can break out of the old belief systems.

### "THEY'RE YOUR PARENTS."

Just because a person is your parent does not mean he has the right to treat you in an abusive or controlling way. And the fact that he is your parent does not mean that you may not need to divorce him just as you would anyone else in your life who caused you continual pain.

> The conviction that parents are always right and that every act of cruelty, whether conscious or unconscious, is an expression of their love is . . . deeply rooted in human beings. . . . (Alice Miller, *For Your Own Good*)

## "Honor Thy Father and Thy Mother."

Why isn't there a commandment to "honor thy children" or at least one to "not abuse thy children?" The notion that we must honor our parents causes many people to bury their real feelings and set aside their own needs in order to have a relationship with people they would otherwise not associate with. Parents, like anyone else, need to earn respect and honor, and honoring parents who are negative and abusive is not only impossible but extremely self-abusive. Perhaps, as with anything else, honoring our parents starts with honoring ourselves. For many adult children, honoring themselves means not having anything to do with one or both of their parents.

## "They're Old [or Sick]."

Adult children of alcoholics or of abusive parents often find that their parents do not "mellow with age" but continue their destructive behavior. In fact, abusive/alcoholic parents often become more destructive over the years as they become even more entrenched in their denial and anger.

Many people think they should excuse those who are sick or old, that somehow these people aren't responsible for their behavior, but being old or sick does not excuse abusive or controlling behavior. While being sick is certainly stressful and can bring out the worst in anyone, it is interesting to note that sometimes those who suffer the most do so graciously and without becoming abusive to others. If a person was kind and loving when she was young and healthy, she is inclined to be the same when old and sick. Those who have always been abusive only become more so when they are old and sick.

## "Forgive and Forget."

The notion of divorcing a parent is taboo in our society. No matter how cruel or unreasonable a parent has been, the adult child is expected to be forgiving. No matter how unchanging the parent continues to be, the responsibility for change always seems to lie on the shoulders of the adult child. And no matter how uncompromising the parent, the adult child is expected to make endless compromises in order to "get along" with that parent. Making peace with our parents is possible for some people, but for many others, to do so would mean not only selling themselves out but also jeopardizing their emotional well-being.

As discussed earlier in this book, some therapists make the mistake of encouraging all of their clients to forgive and forget. What a grave disservice this is! These clients are being asked to do the impossible, and they thus end up feeling hopeless and "bad."

Many people will criticize your decision to divorce a parent because they believe you should be able to forgive. You may hear such messages as this: "God taught us to forgive. If Jesus could forgive us our sins, why can't you forgive your mother or father? Have you never done anything you needed to be forgiven for? Are you perfect? Who are you to judge?"

Sonya would sink onto a deep depression every time her husband's family would lecture her about forgiving her father. She believed strongly in forgiveness because she was deeply religious, but in her heart she knew she just wasn't ready to forgive. She was still too angry at her alcoholic father, who had beaten her mercilessly when she was a child and who continued to drink and to abuse her mother. She felt guilty for not being able to forgive, for not being more spiritual and magnanimous.

Don't let others make you feel guilty because you haven't forgiven your parent. There is no shame in not forgiving; few people ever really complete the task, even when they want to. And for many, "forgiving" can just be a way of denying and pretending that nothing ever happened.

## "That's Just the Way They Are— Why Can't You Just Accept Them?"

Just because we know that a parent has always acted in a certain way doesn't mean that we have to accept it. Abusive behavior is *never* acceptable, no matter whose behavior it is, why he or she behaves this way, or how long the behavior has been going on.

## "But Your Parent Is Such a Wonderful Person!"

It is difficult enough to divorce a parent even when others recognize that the parent is cruel, selfish, or abusive. But when the parent is successful at putting up a facade to the outside world, it makes divorcing that parent especially difficult. Very often I hear clients say, "People can't understand why I would want to divorce my mother. Most people think she's a wonderful person. She's always the first one to help those in need. And she's so charming—people just love her. How can they possibly understand how cruel and ungiving she is to her own family?"

While it is important to make sure you aren't seeing your parent as "all bad," recognize that your parent may have been so successful at hiding her bad side from the outside world that others outside the family may have a hard time seeing your parent as anything but "all good."

### How to Deal with Criticism

Many of your family members and friends will simply not understand what you are doing and will try to talk you out of divorcing your parent, "for your own good." Others may be more overtly critical, strongly reprimanding you for taking such action. Even if you feel you have to divorce a parent for your very survival, you may be criticized and judged harshly.

Those who do not come from dysfunctional families often cannot understand the agony some adult children go through in trying to come to terms with their parents and coping with their ongoing destructive behavior. These adult children are frequently judged and criticized by people who have had totally different experiences growing up and who see them as simply ungrateful, selfish, stubborn, or lacking in respect.

Some criticism will come from unexpected places, places from which you might expect more support. A good example of this is the kind of criticism many experience from their peers in Twelve-Step recovery programs. AA teaches forgiveness and strongly encourages members to understand that parents were victims as well, that they did not intentionally try to hurt their children but were acting out of their own hurt and disturbance. Clients of mine who have spoken with AA friends about divorcing their parents have sometimes been sharply criticized for not being forgiving and for judging.

You may find that outright criticism may not hurt as much as insinuation and subtle denigration, which can cause you to doubt yourself and become confused. With practice, you can learn to anticipate these putdowns and find tactful yet effective ways of dealing with them. In order to help prepare you for this, I have made the following list of some of the subtle criticisms you are most likely to hear, along with some suggestions for how to respond.

☐ *"You should try to understand that your parent was abused and mistreated by her own parents."*
Response: "Yes, my parent probably was abused by her parents, and she in turn perpetuated the cycle of abuse by being abusive to me. That is precisely why I need to divorce myself from her. I need to break the cycle of abuse, and the only way I've found it to be possible is to not be around her. When I'm around my mother she continues to abuse me, and in turn I tend to be either abusive to others or to myself. Understanding why she was abusive doesn't take away the pain and damage she has inflicted on me, nor does it excuse her behavior."

☐ *"Stop judging her—she did the best she could."*
Response: "My parent is the only one who truly knows whether she did the best she could. It is not for me to judge. Whether she did the best she could based on her history and limitations is not the issue here. The real issue is that whether it was her best or not, it was not good enough. I do not deserve the kind of treatment I have received from her, and I do not have to put up with it."

☐ *"No parent is perfect. How would you like it if your children divorced you?"*
Response: "If I treated my own children the way I've been treated, they would have the right to their anger. I hope I

would be a big enough person to listen to their anger and take responsibility for my actions."

☐ *"It happened a long time ago. Why can't you leave it all behind you and get on with your life? Stop living in the past."*

Response: "I *am* trying to go on with my life, and the best way for me to do this is to divorce myself from a parent who has damaged my childhood and continues to upset and hurt me today. It's hard not to live in the past when your parent is still being as abusive, critical, and neglectful as he was when I was a child. I am hoping that by not being around my parent I won't be constantly reminded of my past, that I'll have a chance to heal, and that I can begin my life anew."

Sometimes, it is best not to tell others about divorcing a parent, as Roxanne learned:

Whenever I've talked about divorcing my parents in the past, I've felt extremely defensive. I'm sure it's because right away people who don't understand attack me verbally, as though I've done something to hurt them. The most famous lines are "How could you do that to your own flesh and blood?" and "How could you do that to your poor mother?" So I've learned to keep it to myself unless someone asks. Then I'm as honest as I can be, as long as I can also protect myself in the process. The exceptions, of course, have been those who know me and understand the hell I've been through with my family.

## Telling Your Family

It will be very important for you to tell the rest of your immediate family about your intention to divorce one or both of your parents. They have a right to know, but more important, you have a right to have your intention honored. If you are "emotionally" divorcing a parent but agreeing to still see him at family gatherings, it won't be as important to let your siblings and other family members know about the divorce. But if you are going to "physically" divorce your parent as well, you need to make that clear to your family. You can go into as much or as little detail as you want, but the important thing is that you make it clear that you do not wish to be around your parent.

For example, your family members will need to know that if they invite your parent to a function they need not invite you, because you will not attend if your parent is there. They will need to plan on entertaining you separately from your parent.

As I've mentioned, family members will often be critical of your decision or will try to reason with you or talk you out of it. Often, individual family members will side with the parent you are divorcing and may in turn divorce you. This happens most often with the parent you are not divorcing; she may choose to side with her mate no matter what he has done. You probably won't be surprised if this happens, anyway, since most adult children realize that their parents have banded together in their denial. In some cases, an adult child's entire family will turn against her when she tells them that she is divorcing a parent.

## When Siblings View You As the Enemy

It is more than likely that everyone else in your family has also been damaged by the parent you wish to divorce and by the dysfunctional family system. Nevertheless, others may be in far more denial about how they have been affected than you have ever been. Usually, there is one child in the family who seems to be the one to stand up and confront the abuse, neglect, or alcoholism in the family. Siblings often accuse this person of being disloyal to the parent, of making trouble, of refusing to let bygones be bygones, and of constantly harping about the past. They may see her as the crazy, neurotic, or troubled one—yet, ironically, this child is often the healthiest and strongest one of all. She is the one who has had the courage to face the truth about the family, to seek professional help for her problems, and to confront her abusers. Ultimately, she is the one who has so much determination to recover from her childhood that she is willing to do anything that will help her to heal and flourish—including divorcing herself from a parent.

Siblings can, unfortunately, be the least supportive of anyone. They may be so threatened by your attempts to recover and by the truths that you are uncovering that they actually view you as the enemy. You are taking away their illusions, causing them to doubt their perceptions, threatening to yank them out of their denial. They simply can't afford to listen to you, to take in what you have to say. They can't believe you when you tell them what your parent has done to hurt you and damage you, because then they would have to face the damage that was done to them.

Even a sibling whom you know for certain was also abused by your parent may deny her own abuse and become angry at you for accusing your parent. The fact that you may have actually witnessed the abuse or that she may have previously confided in you about being abused by the parent will bear no weight.

In addition to denial, siblings may have entirely different perceptions about the family and their childhood. Even though they did indeed experience the very same things you did—emotional, verbal, physical, or sexual abuse—they may have perceived the situation very differently. This may be so because they played a different role in the family or developed a different way of coping with the family problems. In addition, your birth order may also have affected your perceptions of the family. Abusive or alcoholic parents can become progressively worse, causing younger children to suffer much more severely than older ones. Or, the reverse can be true—for example, when a parent stops drinking, seeks help for her problems, or has a religious conversion, she may end up treating the younger children better. Sometimes parents favor one child over another or dislike one child more than the others. Any of these variables can contribute to different perceptions among siblings of what their childhood was like.

Sometimes siblings feel so guilty about the way your parent treated you that they simply cannot relate to you honestly. Your sibling may feel guilty because he failed to protect you from your parent or because he didn't tell someone about what was happening to you. Some even feel guilty because they knew you were being abused but secretly felt relieved that it wasn't them.

It is also important to realize that your siblings may still be terribly afraid of your parent and therefore unable to support you.

Keep in mind how long it has taken you to break away from your parent, how hard you have had to work to get over your fears of him. If your siblings have not received any help in the form of therapy or Twelve-Step programs, they are probably just not equipped to face your parent's rage. Even though they are adults, they may still be so hooked into your parent, so afraid of his rage, that they cannot support you for fear of making your parent angry with them.

For whatever reason, your siblings may not only be unsupportive of your decision to divorce your parent but may also perceive it as an insult or threat to them. They may attack you, perhaps even threatening to divorce you unless you reconsider. As unfortunate as it would be to lose a sibling along with losing a parent, don't let yourself be blackmailed. Do what is right for you, and hope that your sibling will eventually come around to your way of thinking or at least become tolerant of your position.

### Telling Your Children

You will need to tell your children about your intention to divorce your parent. Children are naturally very perceptive, and they have probably already sensed that something is going on with you. You have very likely been acting angry or distracted, and they may have overheard conversations you have had with your parent or with others. Children often assume that whatever is wrong with their parent is their fault, so you need to explain what is going on so they won't blame themselves for your unhappiness. It is also important to tell your children why you are discontinuing their visits to their grandparent, because by not telling them you are protecting the abuser and reinforcing secrecy as a family pattern.

Again, tell them only as much as you feel comfortable with. Some people feel that their children should know the reasons for the divorce, while others think it is necessary only to tell them that a divorce has occurred. If your parent was sexually abusive to you and one of the reasons you are divorcing him is to protect your children from being abused by him, it might be important to tell your child about her grandparent's abusive nature in order to further protect her. This is especially true if you are going to allow your child to continue seeing her grandparent.

If you tell your child about your own sexual abuse, be careful to talk to her in ways that are appropriate to her age. If your child is under eight years old you do not need to go into detailed descriptions; instead, tell her in a general way what happened to you. For example, you might say, "Your grandfather hurt me when I was a little girl. I'm afraid he might hurt you in the same way, so I have decided that we should stop seeing him. That is why we are not going over to his house anymore, and that is why I have been crying. If I seem sad, it doesn't have anything to do with you."

If your child wants to know more, she will ask. She may ask you, "How did he hurt you?" In that case, you might want to go into more detail, gearing your answer to your child's age. You might want to just say, "He touched my private parts" or "He got really angry and hit me." If your teenager asks, "What did grand-father do that was so terrible?" you might say, "He raped me" or "He used to physically abuse me."

In general, just provide the information you feel your children need in order for them to understand what is going on and to be protected. Answer their questions honestly, but don't overwhelm them with aspects of the abuse they might not be able to deal with. By all means, make sure you don't use them as a place to dump all your feelings about your parent.

If you are not ready to go into detail about what your parent did or why you want to divorce him, be honest about it. Say that you are not comfortable yet in talking about it, but that perhaps when your child is older or when you become more comfortable with your feelings, you will be able to explain exactly what happened.

Even if your children are adults, it is still important to tell them about the divorce and the reasons for it. Don't expect them to be supportive of your decision or even understanding about your pain. Remember, you are talking about their grandparent, someone they probably love very much. If your children don't want to hear any more about your abuse or about the truth of their grandparent, don't force them to. It will take them some time for them to assimilate what you have told them.

### PROTECTING YOUR CHILDREN

If you were abused by one or both of your parents and you have any fear that they might also abuse your children, you have a right to refuse to allow them access to your children. If your children still want to see your parent they may do so when they become old enough and mature enough to protect themselves from your parent. Until then, you need to afford them the protection they deserve, no matter how they feel about it.

It is painful for everyone concerned to spoil a child's image of his grandparent and to deprive him of having a grandparent, but his safety is far more important. You do not owe your parent the opportunity to have a relationship with your child.

Some adult children feel that it is okay to allow their children to visit their grandparents as long as the visits are carefully supervised. This is especially true when the parent has not been sexually or physically abusive. On the other hand, your children may still encounter behaviors that are unacceptable to you, such as being told not to cry, being forced to eat everything on their plates, or being ridiculed, tickled, or teased. In general, if you have had to go to the extreme of divorcing your parent, he is probably not the kind of person you will want to have influencing your own children.

### WHEN YOUR CHILDREN PRESSURE YOU

No matter how much your children pressure you or how much you are criticized by others for depriving your children of their grandparent, remember that it is your responsibility to take control and to make the decisions when it comes to your children's safety.

Jill's nine-year-old son Adam, gave her a hard time because he wanted to see his grandmother. Even though Jill had explained to him in detail why she was divorcing her mother and why she didn't want Adam to see her, he didn't seem to understand and would nag her constantly to let him see his grandmother. Jill would periodically wonder whether she was doing the right thing. After all, her mother had always been good to Adam, and in fact had tended to spoil him—a far cry from her treatment of Jill when Jill was a child.

But Jill didn't like the way her mother tried to manipuluate her into giving in to Adam's pleas. It just felt like more of her games, and Jill refused to play. She had asked her mother not to call her house anymore, but she would call when Jill wasn't there and talk to Adam, asking him to try to talk his mother into letting him come over. Finally, Jill couldn't stand the pressure any longer. She changed her phone number so that her mother couldn't continue to call. She felt strongly about not having her son see his grandmother, and she didn't want him in the middle any longer.

Some children accept their parents' decisions better than others do. Anna's two children each reacted differently when she told them that their grandfather had sexually abused her, and that for this reason she didn't want them to see him again while they were still young.

My daughter, who is 12, was very upset but understood. My son, 9, just couldn't believe that his grandfather was a child molester, and he accused me of making it up. He told me that I couldn't stop him from seeing his grandfather. We had a big fight over it, and he even stopped talking to me for a few days. But I kept at him to tell me about his feelings, and eventually he opened up a little more. I let him know that I understood how he felt and that I was sorry that he was being deprived of his grandfather. But I also let him know that I wasn't going to back down.

I asked him to think about what he might do if he were in my shoes, if he were a parent in this situation. He thought long and hard, and finally he conceded that he might do the same thing out of concern for his kids. He let me know, though, that he still loved his grandfather, and that when he became an adult he was going to see him. I told him that I didn't want to take away his love for his grandfather, and that if he still wanted to see him when he was 16, that I would let him.

Many clients have discovered that if their children are very small during the divorce, they soon forget about the grandparent if they don't see him for a while. They might ask about him occasionally, but unless the grandparent continues to call or otherwise pressure the children into coming over, they soon adjust to not seeing him.

You will, of course, need your spouse to back you up when you tell your children they cannot see their grandparent. Fortunately, most spouses understand their mate's fears that the children will be abused by the grandparent. If your spouse is having a difficult time understanding your fears, he probably just needs more education about the cycle of abuse. Have him read books on the subject of child abuse so he will better understand. If this doesn't work, there may be other reasons why your spouse refuses to support you. It may be that he was abused by his parent and is in denial. In any case, if you encounter an inordinate amount of resistance from your spouse, there are issues between the two of you to work out, perhaps through marriage counseling.

Some adult children who have divorced a parent have allowed their children to see their grandparent but have regretted it later. Sometimes the grandparent tries to use the children to manipulate the adult children or to get back at them. Some children return home from a visit to a grandparent behaving in a hostile or argumentative manner, a clear reflection of the grandparent's "propaganda." Unfortunately, allowing your children to see their grandparent often puts them in the middle. They have heard negative things about their grandparent from you, and at the grandparent's house they may hear negative things about you.

Until your children are mature enough to take care of themselves, you are the only one who can know what is best for them. They may think you are cruel for depriving them of their grandparent, but it is far more important for you to protect them from harm than it is to let them do what they want. If you have any fears that your children will be abused by the same person who abused you, you have an obligation as a parent to protect them. In addition, you will be breaking the cycle by not allowing another generation of children to pass on the legacy of abuse that has plagued your family.

## YOUR OWN WORST CRITIC: HOW TO HANDLE THE PRESSURES FROM WITHIN

In addition to the pressures you will feel from others, you will also experience self-imposed pressure. Feelings of guilt and doubt will plague you from time to time and cause you to question your decision. There will always be pressure from others, and there will always be holidays and perhaps illnesses to stir up the embers of your smoldering guilt. But you don't have to *act* on your guilt feelings. Acknowledge them, recognize them for what they are, try to balance them with some reality, and then let them die out. Don't let your guilt trap you into putting your needs aside in order to take care of a parent who may not even appreciate the gesture.

### The Burden of Guilt

No matter what your parent has done to you, and no matter how justified you feel in divorcing her, you will undoubtedly feel guilty about doing so. While part of this guilt will come from external pressures, you will also feel guilt from within—the kind of guilt we feel when we don't really think we've done anything wrong but are afraid we have somehow hurt someone else anyway. As angry as you have been at your parent, as much hate as you sometimes feel toward her, you will always love her. Even if your parent hasn't shown any sign of pain because of the divorce, you may assume she is hurting. You may feel that your parent is too proud to show it or too stubborn to beg but is nevertheless hurt.

Some parents are so cut off from their feelings, however, that they don't allow themselves to feel even the slightest amount of pain over their child's decision to divorce them. Instead, they stay stuck in their pattern of always blaming other people for their problems, staying angry instead of feeling their pain.

Some parents, of course, *are* hurt by their adult child's decision to divorce them. It is especially difficult to hold your ground if you hear that your parent is taking the divorce hard. After all, you are not used to standing up for yourself in the first place, much less putting your own needs ahead of someone else's. The kind of guilt that comes from putting your own needs first for a change can be tremendously difficult to deal with. After a lifetime of taking care of others at the expense of your own well-being, knowing that someone else is hurting because of something you did can be overwhelming. But unless you have also heard that your parent has changed tremendously, and unless you have real reason to believe that this is true, resuming the relationship can be a real step backward in terms of your own personal growth.

If you can give yourself some time to adjust to your new way of being, to get used to taking care of your own needs first, you will soon stop feeling guilty for taking care of yourself. Remember, you have given your parent many chances to change. She is responsible for her own actions and inaction. You do not owe her another chance, and you certainly do not owe her another opportunity to hurt you again.

Part of working through your guilt will be realizing that your parent has a separate life from you and a totally separate identity other than just being your parent. While it seems as though adult children from dysfunctional families should understand this better than most people, surprisingly, they sometimes have the hardest time recognizing this fact. Even though your parent clearly saw herself as more than just your mother as evidenced by her lack of caring, attention, supervision, or guidance, you may think of her only in terms of her role as a mother. To counter this think of all the other people and things she put before you and your welfare.

A friend's insight helped Chris deal with her feelings of guilt about divorcing her mother:

> Whenever I thought of my mother, I would picture her sitting all alone in her house, watching television to keep her company. I felt so sorry for her, and I felt like such a rat for abandoning her as I did. Then a friend who grew up with me reminded me of how my

mother would leave me alone even when I was a little girl so that she could go out with some guy. She said, "Don't you remember that your mother always had a boyfriend? What makes you think she doesn't now?" That brought me to reality and out of my self-imposed guilt. Of course my mother was not alone; she never had been. She wasn't pining away for me—she was going on with her life, just like I should be doing!

Another way of working through your guilt is to gain a more realistic picture of just how important you are to your parent. Many adult children overestimate their importance to their parents, somehow forgetting just how unimportant they were to them as children. Your parent may have been "too busy" to help you with your homework or to play with you. Perhaps she didn't seem to notice when you were unhappy, ignored symptoms of the sexual abuse you were suffering, or left you with people who abused or neglected you. She may have neglected your needs for affection, proper nutrition, or medical and dental care. In any of these events, you clearly occupied a far less important place in her life than you may be willing to acknowledge. While your parent may indeed be heartbroken because of the divorce, it is also possible that it hasn't had much of an impact on her at all. And, as mentioned earlier, some parents are actually relieved at not having to deal with a "troublesome" child again.

Even if your parent doted on you and made you the center of her life, it is important to remember that she probably didn't do it so much out of love as out of a fear of reaching out to others or a need to control someone completely. Now that you are not in her life, she has probably been forced to reach out to others or has found someone else to control.

The guilt you might feel because you are depriving your children of their grandparent can evoke another internal twinge. In reality, however, it is your *parent* who is depriving your children of a grandparent, since it is because of his actions that you must keep your children away from him. And while you are facing reality, ask yourself. Just what am I depriving my children of? It is true that your children don't have their grandparent in their lives, but they also don't have the negative influence, the abuse, or the criticism. Maintaining family ties for the sake of tradition does not help your children. It is better that your children do not have a grandparent at all than one who might cause them harm.

For a good while, holidays and birthdays will be "guilt days." It will be almost impossible for your parent's birthday, Mother's Day, Father's Day, or Christmas to go by without your feeling some guilt because you are not with your parent or haven't sent a card or present. "The first Mother's Day that went by without my sending my mother a card was extremely difficult," said Randy, who had divorced his mother a year and a half before.

> I felt like such a bad person, such an ungrateful son. This simple act of not sending a card marked a milestone in my recovery, however. I had always sent a card out of obligation or guilt, not out of any genuine feeling of caring. Although I felt some momentary guilt, I got over it quickly when I thought about what Mother's Day is supposed to represent: it is a day set aside to honor your mother for all the wonderful things she has done for you. I realized that I didn't have any of the feelings you're supposed to have toward your mother—gratitude, admiration, respect, and caring. I stopped feeling guilty when I realized that if I had sent a card it would have been an act of hypocrisy, not a genuine outpouring of affection.

Your parent's birthday can be another time when guilt can overtake you. Carmen always felt especially guilty when her mother's birthday came around:

> I felt guilty for years after I divorced my mother for not seeing her or at least not sending her a present or card. Then last year I reminded myself of how little my mother had ever done for me and how many of my birthdays she had ruined by getting drunk, making a fool of herself in front of my friends, and berating me in front of them. I remembered all the birthdays when I'd ended up crying in my room at night, wishing I'd never been born. This year I didn't feel a bit guilty for not celebrating her birthday. And I made sure *my* own birthday was the best one I've ever had!

### WHEN A PARENT IS SICK OR DYING

Many people are discouraged from divorcing a parent because he or she is sick or dying. This was Judy's situation. "I wanted to divorce my mother," she told me, "but I was afraid she would die and I would regret having divorced her. She was sick, you know, and she could have died anytime. I just couldn't shake my fears of her dying alone. No one deserves that. She'd pushed everyone else away but me."

Judy agonized for several weeks over the decision of whether to divorce her mother. She, like many adult children, was in a painful dilemma, feeling resentful that she couldn't tell her mother exactly how she felt and guilty for even thinking about divorcing a sick woman. Finally, she decided to divorce her. "I couldn't continue to live my life being afraid of how I *might* feel. If she dies, she dies. On the other hand, she has been sick before and recovered, only to make my life miserable again. She is so tough and mean she could outlive us all."

It is almost impossible not to feel some guilt, however fleeting, when your divorced parent is sick or dying. You may blame yourself, thinking that is you hadn't divorced him, he wouldn't have gotten so sick, or you may entertain the fantasy of going to see him and therefore bringing on a miraculous cure.

This kind of guilt is what Judith Viorst calls "omnipotent guilt." In her book *Necessary Losses*, she explains that this kind of guilt rests on the illusion of control, the illusion that we have absolute power over our loved ones' well-being. If a loved one suffers in any way, we irrationally assume that we are to blame. We tell ourselves that if only we had done something differently, we could have prevented his suffering.

Viorst recounts an amusing story about a rabbi who pays two condolence calls on the same day to two different families in which elderly women had died. At the first home, the bereaved son told the rabbi: "If only I had sent my mother to Florida and gotten her out of this cold and snow, she would be alive today. It's my fault that she died." At the second house, the bereaved son told the rabbi: "If only I hadn't insisted on my mother's going to Florida, she would be alive today. That long airplane ride, the abrupt change of climate, was more than she could take. It's my fault that she's dead."

This story reflects how much control we would like to believe we have. But in reality, we have no control over our parents' lives.

Most of us would rather feel guilty than feel our helplessness. By blaming ourselves we allow ourselves to continue to believe that we have life-controlling powers.

Learn to differentiate between real, healthy guilt and neurotic guilt. Healthy guilt occurs when we have violated our own moral code or gone against our own value and belief systems. When we do something that we know is morally wrong, the real guilt we feel serves as a way of discouraging us from doing it again. Real guilt is appropriate to the deed, causing us to feel remorse but not self-hatred.

Neurotic guilt, on the other hand, is usually excessive and misplaced. It can be a way of avoiding your helplessness and powerlessness, as mentioned above, or it can be a by-product of your childhood abuse. Victims of child abuse often feel guilty, ugly, and dirty inside. This feeling of "badness" can rear its ugly head *whenever* you do something that hurts someone else, even if that person deserves it or you are just taking care of yourself.

Remind yourself that you are not divorcing your parent in order to hurt him. If he is hurt as a consequence of your taking care of yourself, you can't help it. It doesn't make you a bad person. Whatever happens to your parent after you divorce him will not be your responsibility or your fault.

Neurotic guilt can also be caused by the withholding of anger that should have (but could not have) been directed toward your parent when you were a child. If you have not released enough of your repressed anger toward your parent for the way he has damaged you, you may end up turning that anger back on yourself. Victims often direct their anger against themselves in the form of guilt.

Adding to your own guilt will be that imposed upon you by the rest of your family. Often, your other parent or your siblings will use guilt to try to pressure you into changing your mind or into visiting your parent. Even though it may be against your better judgment, you may decide to go ahead and see your parent, especially if there is a possibility that he will die soon. If you do break down and visit your parent, make sure that you take care of yourself in the process. And pay attention to your reactions and your feelings while in your ailing parent's presence. They will tell you a lot about your parent, yourself, and whether or not you want to visit him again.

Charlene divorced her father three years ago and had little or no guilt about having any contact with him. Then, last month, her sister called to tell her that her father had had a heart attack and was in intensive care. Charlene agonized for days about whether or not she should go see him. We talked about what her motivation would be to see him, and she acknowledged that it was guilt. We also talked about what she was afraid of and what the possible consequences might be if she did see him. She had divorced her mother at the same time she had divorced her father, and she didn't want to have to deal with both of them at the same time. One of her biggest concerns was running into her mother or her other sister, both of whom were very abusive. Charlene made the decision to go see her father but to stay for only a few minutes and leave if her mother or sister were there.

When she arrived, she was relieved to see that her father was alone but alarmed to see how terrible he looked. Hooked up to a life-support system, he hardly looked anything like she had remembered. They spoke briefly, mostly about how he felt, and then there was nothing else to say. Charlene felt sorry for him, and she even felt some sadness as she got up to say good-bye, knowing that it probably would be the last time she ever saw him alive.

What was so surprising to Charlene was that seeing her father again wasn't as traumatic as she had imagined it might be. She realized that she had done a lot of growing in the intervening three years, and she was no longer afraid of her father. Granted, he was sick, but that had never stopped him in the past from lashing out at her. She had known ahead of time that she was going to take care of herself, whatever that meant. If he had become verbally abusive she knew that she would have had the strength to just get up and leave. She knew she would stay only as long as she wanted to, and not get caught up in any arguing. Charlene was glad she had seen her father, but she realized that she had no interest in seeing him again or in helping to take care of him. When her sister tried pressuring her to see him again, she was able to tell her no without feeling one ounce of guilt.

Charlene had truly divorced herself from her father. She cared about him, but she could remain objective about him and not get hooked back into a negative relationship with him. Even though she had succumbed to internal and external pressures, she knew that her own welfare came first. Many adult children have experiences similar to Charlene's when a parent becomes sick.

Nicole's experience with her ailing father was entirely different.

> Even from his sickbed my father wreaked havoc with my life. He would complain about me to my mother and sisters until they would call me, telling me what a terrible daughter I was for treating my father so poorly. And he was constantly trying to turn my sisters against me by telling them that I had said bad things about them behind their backs. Finally, I couldn't take any more and I divorced him, even though he was terribly sick. I had to take care of myself and put an end to his reign of terror.

Being sick didn't stop Mary's father from divorcing her and thus forcing her to divorce him as well.

> When my father was in the hospital, he made my life and everyone else's a living hell. He complained to the nurses and doctors constantly, and they in turn would complain to me. He had always been rather paranoid, always imagining that people were against him, but it seemed to get worse as he got older. He started supecting that I was trying to kill him. The last straw was when he left instructions with the nurses that I not be allowed to see him because I was giving him drugs to kill him. Fortunately, the nurses didn't believe him, but they did have to follow his instructions.

Some adult children who divorced a parent who has subsequently died feel responsible for the death. If your last contact with your parent was a divorce declaration or an argument of some kind, you may have a tendency to chastise yourself for not having been more understanding and forgiving or, worse yet, to blame yourself for your parent's death. If this happens to you, remember the story the rabbi told, and remember to differentiate between real and neurotic guilt.

On the other hand, if the adult child has successfully divorced a parent and completed the grieving process prior to the parent's death, there is seldom any guilt or, for that matter, any pain. A case in point is B. D. Hyman, daughter of the late Bette Davis. B. D. divorced her mother five years before Davis's death, shortly after having written a book called *My Mother's Keeper*, which revealed how cruel her mother had been to her. In an interview just after her mother's death she was asked, "Do you feel a loss?" B. D. answered, "No, because she hasn't been a part of my life for the past five years. You have to have had something before you can feel a loss."

### Recurrent Doubts

No matter how carefully you worked on your decision-making process and how right your decision to divorce may have seemed at the time, every now and then you will doubt your decision. Perhaps you have been caught off guard because of some unexpected contact with your divorced parent, or you have seen something on television that reminds you of her, or you suddenly miss her for no apparent reason. Then the doubting will begin: "Maybe I was too hasty in my decision," "Maybe I should give her one more chance," "Maybe I am too critical," "Maybe I expect to much," "Maybe she has changed," "I'll regret it if she dies and I never see her again."

This internal questioning is normal and should be expected, but it will usually pass if you give it some time. Whether your doubting is motivated by external pressures or by internal pressures, such as guilt or loneliness, remember that you wouldn't have gotten this far and wouldn't have had to take such an extreme measure unless you had had good reason. Go back over your reasons for wanting to divorce your parent as a reminder that you made the right decision in the first place. In addition, reread Part I of this book to refresh your memory and build up your resolve. If you are still tempted to resume the relationship, note the following:

☐ Your attempt to reconcile with your parent may be just an avoidance of your pain or loneliness or of your need to work on yourself.

☐ Sometimes adult children from dysfunctional families have such an extreme need to be "fair" that they put aside their own needs.

☐ If your parent could not love and appreciate you when you were a little child, how is she going to be able to love you now?

☐ If you are an adult child of abusive parents, it may not be your love but your refusal to grow up that keeps you tied to your parents.

If you find after some time has passed that you genuinely feel you want to try one more time with your parent, then perhaps you will need to do so. Before you attempt a reconciliation, however, make sure you read the last chapter in this book, which discusses reconciliation and how to go about it.

It takes a lot of strength to withstand both the external and internal pressures and not give in, taking what seems like the easier path. But you are not just the victim of a dysfunctional family and abusive parents; you are also a survivor. You have the strength, determination, and courage to withstand any pressure if you keep in mind that you deserve a happy, fulfilling, and healthy life. You've worked so hard to get where you are—don't give up now!

Armed with all of the preceding warnings, all of your preparation, and realistic expectations, the only thing left for you to do is to go through the divorce process itself.

# 6

# Divorcing Without a Lawyer: The Mechanics of Divorce

There are two aspects to divorcing a parent: the internal process of letting go of your parent, which I call the emotional divorce, and the external process of the actual physical divorce. It is inevitable that when you divorce a parent physically—meaning that you end the parent-child relationship, with the intention of never seeing your parent again—you must also divorce him emotionally. On the other hand, you can choose to divorce your parent only emotionally, which means that you cease to feel a close bond with him but opt to maintain some limited contact. You may no longer consider yourself "related" to your parent, but, just as after a marital divorce, you may see your parent sometimes because of your children or other family members and events. In this chapter we will discuss how to go about physically detaching yourself from your parent; in the next chapter, we will address the emotional aspects of divorce.

When you physically divorce a parent you need to sever the ties as completely as possible in order to really feel divorced. Otherwise, you will vacillate, continuing to agonize over whether or not you should try further.

By physically divorcing your parent, you can make a strong statement that you are going to survive without your parent, with-

out his approval and consent—that you are, indeed, going to survive in spite of his rejection and neglect. As Paul Tillich stated in
his book *The Courage to Be,* "The courage to be is the courage to
accept oneself as accepted in spite of being unacceptable."

## THE FORMAL DECLARATION

While some of my clients have not felt the need to make a formal
statement directly to their parents, many have felt it necessary to
do so. In most cases they have wanted to give their parents the
unambiguous message that they don't want any further contact.
Some said they needed to make their intention known formally
because doing this helped them to stand firm with their decision.
Jennifer told me,

> I need to tell my father in writing that I'm divorcing him, because
> this way he won't continue to try to convince me that we can still
> have contact. Otherwise, I know I will continue to back down each
> time he turns on the old charm. This way, he'll know I mean busi-
> ness, and he may be more inclined to stop harassing me so much.
> Putting it in writing will also help me feel stronger in my conviction
> to stay away from him.

Karen went one step further:

> I wrote my dad a letter telling him I was divorcing him. Then I
> changed my phone number and got an unlisted one. I felt finished
> with him, and I didn't want to risk having him call out of the blue
> wanting to discuss it further. I'm glad I did, because I hear from my
> sister that he did try to call and was enraged that I had changed my
> number. He sent me a letter, but that was no problem—I just sent
> it back unopened.

You can make your divorce declaration directly to your parent
through a divorce letter, a formal divorce decree, or in person.
The most common way adult children tell their parents of their
intention to divorce them is through the divorce letter. This is a
letter you compose stating (1) your intention to divorce; (2) your

reasons for divorcing, if you wish to share them; and (3) what this means in terms of future contact, and what connection you wish to maintain, if any. Here is Jennifer's letter:

> Dear Mr. Carter:
> Although you are still legally my father, from this day on I no longer consider you my father, nor do I consider myself your daughter. From this day forward I consider myself divorced from you. I do not wish to ever have any contact with you of any kind. I do not want to see you in person or to communicate with you in any way, including having telephone conversations or corresponding by mail. My mind is made up about this, so there is no need for us to discuss it any further. Please respect my request and my privacy.
> Jennifer Maclaine

And here is Michael's letter to his parents:

> Dear Mother and Father:
> This letter is to inform you that I consider myself divorced from you. You are not the kind of parents I wish to have, since you have made it so clear that I am not the kind of son you wanted. It hurts me to do this, but I must in order to begin to heal from your rejection and to begin my life anew. By divorcing you I give up any hope of having you understand me or stop judging me. I also give up all claim to any inheritance or any assistance from you of any kind. I have made my lawyer executor of my estate and have given him sole authority in case of an emergency, my hospitalization, or my death.
> Michael

Some clients formalize their divorce declarations even more by writing up divorce decrees.

## DECLARATION OF DIVORCE

I, _____ , being of sound mind and body, do hereby claim Final Judgment of Dissolution from _____ , parents of said Petitioner.

The Petitioner, _____ , claims as causes unusual punishment and cruel and malicious treatment from the named offenders. Let it be known that as of _____ , _____ claims no relation to all above-named offenders. The Petitioner, _____ , is under no obligation financially or emotionally to any of the above offenders. The Petitioner, _____ , is granted status as a single person with no immediate relatives. Therefore, the Petitioner, _____ , claims no relationship at all to the above offenders.

Your formal declaration may simply state your intention to be divorced, or it may also include some additional stipulations—for example, that your parent is to have no contact with you in any way, that he or she is to stay away from your children, or that you are not in any way financially responsible for your parent.

Even though you do not need a lawyer to divorce your parent, some people do take legal measures, such as making their wishes known to an attorney or writing up a new will. One woman specified in her new will that she did not want her body buried in the family plot. Some adult children have legally changed their last names or given themselves entirely new names. In rare instances, people have been known to file restraining orders to keep a dangerous parent away.

Some people, like Connie, have simply written a poem to say good-bye:

I loved you, Mama. Mama, I loved you
With all my little heart and all my little soul.
I loved you, Mama,
And you chewed me up and you spit me out.
You hated me.
You despised me.
You detested me.
All because I really and truly loved you.
And I still do.
I still love you.
I'll probably always love you.
But I can't take it anymore.
I'm so tired of trying to believe that you loved me half as much as I
     loved you.
I'm tired of pretending and bending to suit your needs.
You see—I have my own needs.
I need to be loved.
I need to be cared about.
I need what you can't give me.
So I must say good-bye.
God knows, I wanted it to be different between us.
I used to dream of the day you'd come around.
The day my love would overwhelm you.
The day my love would save us.
But my love is not enough.
And your lack of love will kill me if I don't get out while there is
     something left of me.

If you decide you want to make your divorce declaration in
person, practice doing so, in the same way you did earlier when
rehearsing your confrontation or farewell. You can practice with an
empty chair, into a tape recorder, or with a partner filling in for
your parent. As you did with your confrontation, choose a safe

place for your meeting. Know what you are going to say ahead of time, and make sure you say everything you want to say, because this may be the last time you get a chance to talk with your parent. There is no need for discussion—it is too late for that now. Just say your good-bye, and leave.

As mentioned earlier, when we dealt with confrontations, you will obviously not want to make your divorce declaration in person if your parent is dangerous or if there is any chance that you yourself might end up becoming violent.

## DIVORCING A PARENT AFTER HE HAS DIVORCED YOU

Sometimes adult children need to formally divorce their parents because their parents have completely rejected them. Although some parents divorce an adult child when he begins to stand up to them and confront them, as discussed in chapter 3, most often they do so because they cannot accept their child's lifestyle. Whether the child is gay, has married someone the parents disapprove of, done something they don't like, or joined a religion they do not accept, the message these parents give is the same: "Your lifestyle is so abhorrent to us or causes us so much pain or embarrassment that we cannot tolerate being around you."

Kevin, a gay client of mine who had been rejected by both his parents, felt it was necessary to make a formal divorce declaration.

> When my parents stopped talking to me, I felt devastated. I felt like the scum of the earth because my own parents had told me I repulsed them. Divorcing them formally was the best thing I could have done for myself, because by doing so I was making a statement that I was no longer going to be a victim. I was finished with sitting around hoping against hope that someday they might love me for who I am. And I was also no longer going to be a victim of their narrow-minded thinking. I was the one who was taking the action, not just idly standing by while they rejected me and tried to make me feel like I was bad. It took a lot of courage on my part to write it down and mail it to them, but I felt great afterward. I felt incredibly powerful—like I now owned my own power and had taken back my life.

Sara's father was the minister of a fundamentalist church. All of Sara's life, he had warned her about the sins of drinking, dancing, and wearing makeup—all of which would lead to the biggest sin; fornication. When Sara started high school, she found that she felt more and more isolated because of her family's rigid beliefs. She started putting on makeup in the girls' bathroom at school and then taking it off before she left for home. Since her father forbade her to go to school dances, she started lying to him and telling him she was at a friend's house while she went to the dances. Because her father refused to let her date, she started sneaking off to the girls' gym to neck with the boys during and after the school dances. Gradually, she let them go further and further with her, until she finally had intercourse with several boys.

When she became pregnant she was so afraid of her father's wrath that she ran away from home. She lived on the streets for a while, where she met an older girl who befriended her and taught her how to steal and panhandle for a living. Sara missed her family, and as the time drew closer for her to have her baby, she knew she couldn't continue to live as she had been. Finally, she broke down and called her family. She told her mother and father that she was pregnant and begged them to let her come home to have the baby. They refused. Her father yelled at her that she was a sinner and that she had disgraced the family. He told her that she had made her bed and that now she could lie in it, and that he never wanted to hear from her again. This was ten years ago, and Sara has tried to contact her parents several times since, but they still refuse to talk to her. They have never seen their granddaughter.

Even though Sara's parents had essentially divorced her years ago, she now needed to divorce *them.* She needed to give up trying to get back into their good graces. Continually trying to regain their love kept her emotionally bound to them and kept her from going on with her life. Sara decided to write to her parents and officially divorce them as a way of breaking out of the victim role. "I needed to do it so I would stop feeling guilty and bad about myself," she told me. "They were still punishing me for something I did as a teenager! I wanted to go on with my life. I needed to let them go so that I wouldn't continue punishing *myself.*"

If your parent has turned his back on you, it will be important for you to formally divorce him as a way of taking back your power and as a sign that you have given up trying to please him. Otherwise, you will continue to feel like a bad person, and this will affect your self-esteem. You can accomplish the formal divorce through any of the means discussed above. The important thing is that you do it.

## DIVORCING YOUR ENTIRE FAMILY

Some adult children are faced with the difficult task of not only severing all ties with one or both parents but of stopping all contact with their siblings, grandparents, and all other members of their family of origin. This decision is based on their awareness that the entire family is severely dysfunctional, and that the only way to be healthy is to break away from the family altogether. Those who have children often realize that no one in their family is healthy enough for their children to be around. The abuse, alcoholism, neglect, or overcontrol has damaged their siblings to the point at which they are either poor role models for the children or a potential danger to them.

It is not always the adult child who makes the break. Sometimes they are cast out of the family because they dared to talk about the dysfunction, alcoholism, or abuse, or because they reported their parents, grandparents, or siblings to the police or to child-protective services. Having the family secrets exposed may enrage other family members: "How could you report your own father?" "How dare you tell those lies?" "Why couldn't you just keep it within the family, where it should be? We watch him to make sure he doesn't do that anymore—why did you have to bring in the police?"

Whether it is your decision or that of your family members, serving all ties with your entire family is particularly devastating. You will need a long period of time for mourning and readjustment, a time to evaluate your life and discover who you are without your family. For some, this is a time to face their aloneness in the world. Having faced this, they have discovered who they are. Jody expressed this very well when she said, "I had to give up my family in order to find out who I am."

Roxanne told me what it was like to divorce her entire family:

At sixteen, I confronted my Dad about his sexual abuse yet again, only this time with my mother present. He laughed in my face, called me a liar, and challenged me to call the police. I picked up the phone, whereupon he flew across the room and punched me in the face. He then proceeded to convince my mother and brother and sister (who had just walked in the door) that I was a candidate for the nuthouse, sent my brother and sister back out to play and me to my room, and gave my mother some sleeping pills because she was complaining she just couldn't take any more. He then went in to take a shower.

I ran away that day and never went back. That was the end of my abuse but not of the effect it had on my life.

During the next six years, I had a relationship with my mother but only during those periods when my dad had left her. She just didn't want to be alone, so she would pretend to be the ideal mom I had always dreamed of—that is, until my dad came back. Then, once again, I didn't exist for her.

Finally she divorced my dad (but was still seeing him on and off). Three months pregnant with my daughter, I explained to my mother that if she got back together with him, I wouldn't allow her to see or know my children, not out of spite but for my children's safety.

I began to see the real her shortly after our little talk. Along with my brother and sister I had gone to a Christmas party at my mom's office. By this time I had been in counseling for over a year. That night was a real eye opener. The topper was when my mom asked me to entertain her date for the evening because she couldn't stand him anymore. This guy was already getting too close to me and, once again, my mom was pushing me into taking her place with a man. I told her, "You did this to me as a kid, when I had no choice. Now I'm an adult, I do have a choice, and the answer is no!"

After such a crazy night I decided my New Year's resolution would be to limit my time with my mom and to stay away from my brother and sister, who were too far gone into their drug addictions.

Two weeks went by and I hadn't talked to my mom. Normally I

would call her almost every day, but the longer I went without calling her, the better and worse I felt. My husband was amazed that she hadn't called *me*, but it showed me how one-sided our relationship was.

Two months went by and I found out what I had suspected all along—my dad had moved back in with her. I was so glad that this had happened before my daughter was born. My mother had hurt and betrayed me one last time.

Nine months after separating from my family again, my dad blew his head off with a shotgun while drinking at his parents' house. When I was a little girl I had believed that if my dad would just die or go away and never come back we could finally be a happy, normal family. Then everyone would see how much I loved them and that I had been telling them the truth about him all along. Maybe his death came too late, when the family was already too damaged. Maybe my mom was always as sick as my dad but just showed it in a different way.

Six months later, I wrote letters to my mom, her mom, my dad's mom, my brother, and my sister, divorcing everyone individually. I got three responses. My sister responded to the letter I wrote my mother, informing me I was as crazy as my dad and that I belonged in a mental institution. My dad's mom said I should forgive and forget. My mom's mom said she had no idea that I had been abused but still couldn't understand why I needed to break away. She, too, told me to forgive and forget.

It's been three years since I divorced them, and facing the truth about my mother and the fact that she never felt the love for me that I feel for my daughter has been the hardest thing I have had to face so far. Divorcing my family has also meant giving up all hope that they will ever believe me, care about me, or come out of denial. When I divorced my family I was really ready. I had been separated from them for one year. During that year, the longer I was away the better I felt about me and my life. I began to feel good about my choices. I was really glad that my daughter wouldn't know my family, because they would have poisoned her by taking away every precious and beautiful moment I had with her and making it ugly. They would have made me see her as being bad and manipulative. Because of my divorce, I see my daughter as the precious gift she is. I see my husband as the caring person he is.

My family was always in the background waiting to take every happy moment away from me and make it bad. They found something wrong in everything. I wasn't free to be happy or to care deeply about anyone. A year after I divorced my family I quit drinking, thanks to God and to the fact that I didn't need it anymore. I could finally enjoy myself without drugs. I was also free to face the feelings of my childhood and the memories of who these people really were and of how they had treated me as a child. I had a lot of anger, especially toward my mother, that I couldn't get in touch with when I was around her.

There is so much freedom with divorcing my family, but there is pain, too—the pain that they are never going to believe me, never going to get help, never going to love me the way I deserve to be loved. And there is the pain that my children won't have any grandparents to love and cherish them. The pain is there, at some times more than others. But so is the freedom to live my own life and be happy, to make my own decisions, and to really be able to love my children and protect them without someone in my family telling me I'm doing it all wrong, I'm making a big mistake, or that I'm being overprotective.

Connie had a similar experience when she divorced her family.

Divorcing my parents and my sisters has given me a freedom no words can describe. And there are also no words to describe the pain I endured when I separated from them. But if I had to do it again, I wouldn't hesitate for a moment.

I had to get away from them in order to build a brand-new self-image. They had me believing I was worthless, and that is a lie. I couldn't make new friends while I was under their control and manipulation. My relationship with my son improved 110 percent after I divorced my family. I needed space so I could separate what was true about me from their image of me. I feel a great sense of relief, and I have peace of mind because I don't have to pretend that there is love when there isn't.

I'm more in touch with my feelings and my true nature. I feel more confident, more vibrant, more alive. I now have ambitions and goals that are my own, not someone else's. I am able to stand up for myself with other people now. I am more outspoken. And one of the best results of all is that I have a wonderful sense of humor that had been buried. I feel free to have fun now—I didn't feel this way before.

I feel free to be happy, free to be an authentic person. I can have men friends and women friends and not be ridiculed. I have a better job than I ever had in my whole life. I have social activities now that I didn't have the time or energy for before. I used to spend all my time and energy trying to fix my family. My new friends are healthier; I'm no longer attracted to unhealthy people. Saying good-bye to my family was extremely difficult. But it was a matter of life and death for me. My spirit was almost gone. Now I have a very lively, very lovely spirit.

## DIVORCING A PARENT WHO HAS DIED

Just because your parent is dead does not mean that you may not need to divorce him. Jean's father died before she could divorce him, so she had to do so after his death. She did it by actually going to his grave site and having an imaginary conversation with him. She told him she was divorcing him and explained to him why she was doing it. She told him how he had hurt her and damaged her life, and that she had always been afraid of him—so afraid, in fact, that she wasn't able to divorce him until after he died.

Even though her father was obviously already out of her life, the act of divorcing him was incredibly empowering for Jean. She didn't want her father to have any hold on her, not even in his death. She told me,

It feels entirely different to have a parent out of your life because he is dead rather than because *you* have chosen to divorce him. In some ways it felt like a dirty trick to me that my father died before I was ready to confront him. It took away all my power, because even if you don't love someone you feel a sense of helplessness and hopelessness with the act of death itself. But by divorcing him I felt back in control. In a funny way, it made it *my* choice.

Vanessa had temporarily separated from her father two years before he had a recurrence of cancer. She had separated in order to get away from her father's constant criticism, but when she heard he had cancer all that seemed unimportant. She called him up and told him that she would like to reconnect with him again.

He was still hurt from the separation, and in his usual cold and vindictive way he said, "We don't have anything to say to each other." But Vanessa persevered: "I really would like to try again, Dad. I've missed you." He answered, "Well, I didn't miss you." He ended the conversation by saying, "I'll think about it."

Vanessa recalled,

> Even though I was afraid of being hurt, I wanted to do it for *him*—after all, he was dying. About a week later he called from the hospital and said, "I lied to you. I did miss you." I felt very encouraged by this and flew to New York to visit him in the hospital.
>
> It wasn't long before I realized that the relationship had to be on his terms. And it wasn't long before he started to criticize me again, just as he had most of my life. He blamed me for all of our emotional problems—there was no give and take. I also began to realize that I didn't have feelings for him as he was now. All my love was for my memory of the father I'd had when I was six years old—my nice daddy.
>
> When my father died several years later, we were on speaking terms, and I grieved his death. But I was also relieved. It wasn't until after his death that I realized he hadn't been a nice person and that I didn't respect him. He didn't like females, and his dislike for me had been very destructive to my self-esteem.
>
> I wasn't able to divorce him while he was still alive, and I don't regret that. But I realized after he died that I still needed to divorce him, even though he was dead. I needed to finish up my work with him. Writing him a divorce letter was the best thing I've ever done for myself. It really helped me to end the relationship once and for all—and on *my* terms. Just recently, while lighting a mourning candle to commemorate his death, I realized I was glad he was gone.

There are several ways that you can divorce a dead parent. Some of my clients, such as Jean, have conducted grave-side divorce rituals by reading a divorce decree or divorce letter aloud at a parent's grave. This has given them the sense of actually talking to their parent. Others have role-played, talking out loud to an empty chair, to a picture of their deceased parent, or to someone who was willing to take the role of the parent.

As difficult as it may have been to work up to, divorcing your parent physically is soon over. The emotional side to your divorce will take time and will in part involve mourning the loss of your parent, a process that will be discussed in detail in the next chapter.

# CHAPTER 7

# Letting Go: The Process of Emotional Divorce

Often, we do not find out how entwined we are with our parents until we try to separate. Even though you and your parent may have been practically strangers to each other for years, with hardly any contact, you may still be very tied to each other emotionally. And even if you are now physically separated from your parent, you have probably not separated psychologically.

Emotional divorce is a process of letting go. In emotional divorce you let go of any hope of getting what you needed and wanted as a child; you give up the fantasy of what could have been. As painful as it is to cut off all contact with a parent, it can be even more painful to give up the fantasy that someday your parent will come through for you, that he or she will change and finally become a good parent.

As part of emotionally divorcing your parent you must also let go of any further attempts to resolve the conflicts between you or to work on the relationship. In essence, when we divorce our parent emotionally, we are saying: "I will no longer expend any energy on this relationship. I have stopped trying to change the relationship or my parent, and I will stop arguing with him, trying to control him, or trying to understand him or make him understand me. In addition, I will stop feeling responsible for him in any way—emotionally or financially—and will stop expecting him to be responsible for me." As I mentioned earlier, the emotional divorce began long before you ever made your wish to divorce known to your parent, and it will continue throughout the divorce process.

Getting emotionally divorced also means you have to separate from your parent, to *individuate* once and for all. You can finally become you—not an extension or a replica of your parent, but your own unique self. By discovering your own individuality, you can gain enough confidence in yourself that you will no longer feel crushed by your past. It is a time when you face your past and face yourself, a time to sever the emotional bond with the past and to build a new life for yourself. As you gain more control of your own life you will be less afraid of the future. This internal process is what divorcing a parent is really all about. The actual physical separation is merely secondary.

For some, the divorce will be strictly an emotional divorce, since they will continue to have contact with their parent from time to time. Those who accomplish an emotional divorce often find that even though they continue to have some contact with their parent, their emotional investment changes considerably. They don't feel as connected to their parent, as concerned about her feelings, her needs, her reactions to them. If you achieve a successful emotional divorce, you will feel far more objective about your parent, because she will simply not impact you in the same way. When you are with her you will feel very much as though you were in the presence of an acquaintance, someone with relatively little impact on you and your life.

Clients who have successfully divorced a parent emotionally sometimes compare the experience to their actual divorce from a spouse, as in Claudia's case.

> When I first filed for divorce, I found myself very much invested in my ex-husband's reactions. I found it extremely difficult to be around him because I always felt an incredible amount of tension in his presence. Even a phone call about a minor issue could elicit intense feelings of rage and pain. But as time went on and I continued to let go, I found that I could see him or talk to him with less and less emotional upheaval. Finally, as I was able to let go more

completely, I discovered that I could be around him and feel relatively normal, with almost no feeling at all for him.

I went through almost the same process when I divorced my father. I can be detached and objective around him now. I finally gained a real sense of clarity about who my father is, and about what I can and cannot reasonably expect of him. It still amazes me that this person I loved so much before can mean so little to me now, just as it was with my ex-husband. I care nothing about my father's private life—all I am concerned about is how he treats my children and whether he is reasonable and polite with me. But that's what divorce is all about, isn't it?

If you choose to divorce emotionally but not physically, it will be necessary for you to first be as clear as possible about what type of contact you will feel comfortable with, and to then communicate this to your parent. You have a right to decide if, when, and how you want to see your parent. To help you decide this, complete the following sentences until you have no more responses:

I will see my parent if _____ .

Example: . . . *I feel strong enough.*

. . . *my father is not there.*

I will see my parent when _____ .

Example: . . . *I feel ready.*

. . . *I initiate it, not at his request.*

I will see my parent under the following circumstances:

_____ .

Example: *Only at my home.*

*I will not discuss our relationship
any further.*

You may want to send your parent a letter outlining these rules and your expectations of how you want to be treated. For example, you may choose to limit your contact to phone calls or letters, not seeing your parent at all. On the other hand, seeing your parent but not sending any "obligatory" letters or cards may be a significant step for you toward an emotional divorce. Brenda told me,

> I stopped sending my mother cards for birthdays, Christmas, and Mother's Day. For years I had struggled to find a card that said what I really wanted to say, but usually there were none. I'd look and look until I finally found one that would just say "Happy Birthday" or "Happy Mother's Day." All the others were sentimental and said things like, "You are such a loving, giving mother." I couldn't bring myself to send these, because they weren't true. Finally, I realized that I didn't want to send her *any* cards, and it felt so much better to honor my feelings.

## MOURNING THE LOSS OF YOUR PARENT

Emotional divorce from your parent includes the ultimate in letting go—fully mourning the loss of your parent. This means experiencing and dealing with all the emotions this loss creates, and acknowledging and accepting the truth—that the relationship is now over.

Losing a parent is devastating, even if you are the one who has ended the relationship. We feel abandoned even when we are the one who has left. How can one experience years of togetherness, however neurotic or abusive, and not feel the pain of parting? You can't expect to be able to forget a parent who has so imprinted your life just because you have divorced him.

Fortunately, the same determination to live a happier, healthier life that brought you to the decision to divorce your parent will help you to weather the pain of your loss. Whenever it gets too painful, you can use that determination to bolster your strength and help you go on. I still have moments of terrible pain when I think of my mother. The child part of me sometimes still yearns for her (or, more accurately, for a good mother), but these feelings are followed almost immediately by the memory of how terrible I felt in her presence and the realization of how much better I feel since I have stopped seeing her.

Many of you will feel a true sense of loss for the times when there were closeness, love, and support between you and your parent. As discussed earlier, even the most abusive or neglectful parent can sometimes be caring. But even if you have felt little or no closeness to your parent and may initially feel relieved to have him out of your life, you will need to grieve your loss. We experience loss not only when we are deprived of things we have had and valued, but also when we lose things that we had expected or hoped for—or, as Howard Halpern defines them in *Cutting Loose*, the "if onlys":

> In saying good-bye to our parents we are not only bidding farewell to these particular people, but to our link to the past and to our roots. But most poignantly and most frighteningly, we are saying good-bye to the "if onlys." We are saying good-bye to the illusions built on "if only Mom," "if only Dad," "if only the world. . . ." We are facing life as it really is, with no unrealistic hopes and yet whole new exciting possibilities.

You may not even feel the loss of your parent for a while. In fact, you may feel so good to have her out of your life that you may not even realize that you are experiencing a loss. Many people go through a "honeymoon" period after divorcing a parent during which time they feel incredibly free, unburdened, and almost joyous. Others are so in touch with their anger toward their parent that any feelings of sadness or pain at the loss are either buried or overshadowed by the anger.

Some people do not experience a sense of loss until there is a family-oriented holiday or special occasion that pulls at their heartstrings and reminds them of their parent. For example, your first Christmas away from your parent may be the hardest time, especially if you have had to divorce both parents or the entire family. Many adult children have no other family and may not even have any close friends. Going through your first holiday without family can be excruciatingly painful, even when you have very few good memories of family Christmases. And on Mother's Day or Father's Day, depending upon which parent you have divorced, you may experience an almost overwhelming feeling of abandonment.

On the other hand, you may experience a terrible sense of loss almost immediately after you have made your divorce decree. This pain, which I call "orphan pain," can be likened to the feelings of a small child who is all alone in the world, with no one to love him. Some clients have described feeling as though they had a void inside, a huge, empty space where their parent once resided. This can be a terrible feeling, and it will take a lot of courage on your part to stay with your feelings of emptiness and pain and not try to run from them. But as a survivor of an abusive or deprived childhood, you have withstood pain and loneliness before and triumphed over them, and you can do it again.

You may feel so alone and abandoned that you may fear you have made a terrible mistake. At this point it will be important for you to go back over the list of reasons you divorced your parent in the first place, making a commitment to wait at least a month before reassessing your situation. It will be important to remind yourself that in most cases you can always change your mind and try a reconciliation with your parent if you decide that you have, indeed, made a mistake.

But you have come this far, and changing your mind at the first sign of loss and pain is not the best thing to do. Your second thoughts may just be ways for you to avoid pain. Vacillating between not seeing your parent, missing him, and then changing your mind will only confuse you more and weaken your position. We all want to avoid pain, of course, but the price of doing so can be terribly high. If you can stay with the pain, you will soon realize that it hasn't gotten the best of you, and that you are stronger for having endured it and, ultimately, for conquering it.

### The Phases of Grief

Whenever you feel your loss—immediately, after the first rush of freedom has worn off, after your anger has subsided, or when the first important holiday or special occasion occurs—you will need to go through a grieving process in order to let go of your parent.

While adjusting to the loss of your parent, it will be important for you to understand the grief and the grieving process that accompany loss of any kind. Elizabeth Kübler-Ross was the first to describe the stages of grief in relation to death. My phases differ somewhat from hers.

The grief that comes from letting go of a parent is intense, affecting our emotions, our bodies, and our lives in general. Learning to face the reality and the pain of your loss and saying good-bye to your parent is a tremendously difficult process, but it *can* be done. The pain of your loss will eventually subside. Grief is a mixture of emotions—sorrow, anguish, longing, deprivation, regret, anger, and fear. It may be experienced physically as exhaustion, emptiness, tension, sleeplessness, or loss of appetite. In order to complete the grieving process, you will need to face your feelings openly and honestly and then express them fully. When we allow ourselves to feel these painful feelings and we also share the grief with safe and supportive others, we are able to complete our grief work.

Such experts as Kübler-Ross have observed that the typical progression of grief feelings usually starts with shock, followed by denial, anger, depression, insight, and, finally, acceptance. These phases do not necessarily proceed in the same order for everyone, and you may go in and out of each stage. One moment you may feel that the loss is intolerable and that you can't possibly survive it, and the next you may feel strong enough to go it alone. You may face the loss and mourn your parent at one point, only to find later on that you are denying and repressing your feelings of loss. You may be angry one moment, crying uncontrollably the next. Allow yourself to progress through each phase, experiencing all the accompanying feelings. Then you can truly let go and get on with your life.

During the first phase of grief—usually involving feelings of shock, numbness, and a sense of disbelief, which may last for hours, days, or weeks—much of our pain may be shut off, as though we were partially anesthetized. This numbness initially insulates us from the intensity of our feelings and may prevent us from grasping the full significance of our loss.

Sometimes we feel panic and become suddenly afraid that we cannot go on alone. This may cause us to feel like frightened, desperate children, terrified of being all alone, of not being able to survive without our parent. At these times we may begin to see our parent in an unrealistic light, through the eyes of the desperate child instead of the aware adult. When this happens it will be important to comfort your inner child and assure her that she is *not* all alone—that she has you, the adult. Hold her, soothe her, and tell her that you love her. It is also important at this time to reach out to supportive others.

While we are in this shock phase our sorrow and pain are often hidden from us, but our anger may burst forth unexpectedly at almost any target. Be careful that you do not take your anger out on innocent people. Instead, focus your anger on your divorced parent as a way of reinforcing your decision. At the same time, be aware that anger may be one of the few outlets you have for the disbelief, helplessness, and frustration you feel when confronted with this loss. Allow yourself to be angry over your loss, but know that underneath the anger lie your sorrow and pain.

After this first, relatively short phase of mourning, we move to the second and longest phase, that of intense psychic pain and disorganization, which may last for months. When the shock wears off we begin to experience the full impact and pain of facing our loss. In her book *Life Is Victorious!*, Diane Kennedy Pike described the loss of a loved one as being similar to having a tree that had been growing in one's heart suddenly yanked out by the roots, leaving a gaping hole or wound.

It is natural in this phase for you to cry a great deal.

While the pain of the loss may seem unbearable at times, and you may feel that you can't withstand the pain, keep telling yourself that you are going to get through this phase—because I assure you that you will.

In addition, you may ruminate over the lost relationship, over memories, over your last encounter with your parent, and over unfinished business. This ruminating is simply a part of the healing process. You may also feel blank, "spaced out," unable to concentrate, or focus. At the same time, you may be overwhelmed by feelings of acute pain, bitterness, anger, self-pity, and guilt, and by a sense of impoverishment or emptiness.

It is inevitable that you will feel depressed while grieving the loss of your parent. Depression can cause us to feel irritable, apathetic, withdrawn, unresponsive, unable to concentrate, powerless, and insecure, and to experience a loss of appetite and extreme fatigue. All of these reactions are quite normal and should be expected. On the other hand, severe depression may cause us to fell self-destructive or even suicidal. While it is also natural to have these feelings from time to time, if you become afraid that you could actually act on these feelings, contact a professional therapist right away or call your local suicide-prevention hot line.

Almost everyone who faces a loss has some difficulty sleeping. This difficulty, which may involve insomnia, fitful or restless sleep, or disturbing dreams, is a result of the intense strain brought on by the psychological work involved in grief. Even in normal times we all tend to work out many of our problems during sleep. Dreams are an important way of reexperiencing and working through emotionally charged experiences, and of problem solving.

Amber had recurrent dreams about her mother for several months after divorcing her: "Often in the dreams we are together, and we're happy. I wake up and realize it will never be, and I become terribly sad."

Nightmares are often more prevalent when we are grieving. Julie started having nightmares about her father shortly after she divorced him. One such nightmare was particularly frightening:

I dreamed my father had come to get me to take me home. When I refused to go with him, he became extremely angry with me and started pulling my hair and slapping me. I fought back the best I could, but he was stronger than me and overpowered me. He pulled me by my hair all the way to his car. I was so afraid he was going to get me in his car, and then I knew it would be all over. I woke up screaming and crying hysterically. I scared my husband to death. When he tried to comfort me, I slugged him before I realized who he was. Then he just held me and let me cry. I was afraid to go back to sleep and lay awake the rest of the night, half expecting my father to come to my door to get me.

You will inevitably have feelings of loneliness and yearning, and you will feel a painful gap in your life. But allowing yourself to feel this loneliness, however painful, indicates that you are allowing yourself to acknowledge the truth of the loss. As you heal, these feelings will lessen.

The feeling of abandonment is one of the most agonizing feelings we must endure and conquer in grief. Even though in this case *you* are the one who has done the leaving, the child inside you understands only that she feels abandoned. She will feel deserted, unwanted, and unloved. Again, it will be crucial that you take the time to reassure your inner child, nurturing and comforting her as you learned to do in chapter 4.

We now move toward what is called the "completion" of mourning. And while there will still be times when we weep for, long for, and miss our parent, completion means that an important degree of recovery, acceptance, and adaptation has been achieved.

During this last phase of grief you may need more quiet time and fewer people around you. Or, if you have been very quiet and withdrawn, you may now be ready to come out of your self-imposed isolation and resume a more active social life. You may feel the need for more fulfilling activity and more involvement in life. As a sign of your recovery you will notice that you are more invested in and focused on the future than the past.

You will also see that you are moving closer to recovery from grief when your divorced parent is no longer your primary focus. As your sense of loss diminishes, moving from intense sorrow to mild sadness, your sleep, appetite, energy, and functioning will be restored to near normal.

Even though you may be inclined to think that your mourning is over because you have more energy and feel better able to cope, your need to express your emotions continues during this period. You may still be working through your grief as intensely as before, although in more subtle, less obvious ways. And there may be difficult days even after the full thrust of mourning is complete. This reemergence of grief is a natural part coming to terms with a loss.

## A Time for Grieving

Completing the grieving process takes time. Generally, the greater the loss, the longer the the process takes. For a major loss, such as the loss of a parent, the time required for the healthy completion of grieving is usually one year or more. In fact, many cultures and religions designate one year as the time for mourning following a death. This is not only because it may take that long to recover from the loss, but also because in one year we are able to experience all of the holidays and special occasions, such as birthdays and anniversaries, without the loved one and thus learn to adjust to her absence.

Some people will need a longer period of time than others to mourn, and for some the mourning process will be exceptionally painful. Those who have had to divorce both parents or their entire family will obviously be among those who have the most difficult time. And when the divorced parent is the adult child's last living parent or relative, the loss can have a particularly profound impact. If you have been fortunate enough to start a new family of your own—if you have a spouse and children, or a surrogate family of friends and other supportive people—chances are that your grieving process will not be quite as excruciating. But if you are alone, with no mate and no replacement family, your time of grieving will be especially trying.

In my case, my mother is really the only family I have. I never knew my father and so have not had any contact with that side of my family. My mother's parents both died before I was born, and I have no siblings. Two of my uncles are dead; I have an aunt who lives out of state whom I have seen only once in my life, and I have an alcoholic uncle whom no one has heard from for years.

When I divorced my mother, I truly felt like an orphan who was all alone in the world. Since I have no children of my own, I now essentially had no family. While this made me especially value the surrogate family I had created for myself, at the same time the awareness that I had no family whatsoever left me with a very empty feeling. I walked around with a deep sense of sadness and loss for over a year, crying at any movie that even hinted at loss.

Things are especially difficult for me on holidays, when I spend time with other people's families. Even though I never had a good holiday with my mother, there was at least the feeling that I was with my family. I have been divorced from my mother for almost two years now, and last Christmas I had the best Christmas I ever had. I didn't miss my mother or feel guilty that I hadn't visited her. I bought myself a new puppy, and I began the new year feeling hopeful and in charge of my own life.

It may be surprising to you to realize how much pain and abandonment the divorce causes you to feel even when you have not been close to your parent, but it is important to admit your feelings and not deny them. Emotional pain seems endless only when all of our energy is spent in suppressing our feelings.

Because we cannot tolerate the continual onslaught of emotional pain, the natural process of grieving involves time of intense feeling followed by periods of quiet. Allow yourself to move naturally in and out of your pain; do not try to control your feelings either way. If you confront your grief rather than avoid it, you will shorten the length of time it will take you to mourn.

To work through the pain of grieving, we need to experience our feelings as they come up, without trying to change them. These feelings are often so painful that we may try to avoid them in the following ways:

- [ ] continuing to deny the loss
- [ ] intellectualizing about it
- [ ] adopting a macho mentality (I'm strong, I can handle it by myself)
- [ ] using alcohol or drugs

☐ overeating or engaging in some other type of compulsive behavior (such as shopping or gambling)

☐ making vain attempts at reconciliation

While we may get temporary relief by using such methods, when we avoid feeling our grief we only prolong our pain. If you are a recovering alcoholic or drug addict, you will need to be especially careful not to revert back to your old habit of numbing your pain by using drugs or alcohol. There will undoubtedly be times when you will be tempted to use again, especially when the pain seems to be unbearable. During these times, make sure you reach out to your sponsor and that you attend extra meetings until you get over the crisis.

Take the time to grieve. Cry as often as you need to. Tears have natural healing powers, both physiologically and emotionally. With each tear that you cry you will be healing your mind, soul, and body of the pain, not only of the loss of your parent, but of all of your losses, big and small. Don't be surprised if you find yourself crying at old movies, old songs, at things you read—anything that reminds you of your parent or your childhood. As Margie told me, "It happens when I least expect it—I can be driving in my car or doing the grocery shopping and hear an old song on Muzak, and suddenly I burst out crying."

Make sure that your living environment and the people with whom you associate will support rather than inhibit or discourage your grieving. During your time of grieving, companionship may become your greatest need. You will need others to listen to you, talk to you, or hold you. If you have no one available to you, this may be a good time for you to seek professional help or to join a support group or Twelve-Step program, such as Adult Children of Alcoholics or Al-Anon. Grief can be naturally healed if we have support. According to Jane Middelton-Moz and Lorie Dwinell in their book *After the Tears,* "One of the things we know about grief resolution is that grief is one of the only problems in the world that will heal itself with support. The reason people go into delayed grief is that there's nobody there to validate and support them. You cannot grieve alone. Millions of us adult children tried it. We went to sleep crying into our pillows or locked in the bathroom."

Divorcing a parent causes us to feel our aloneness in the world. As important as it is to have the support of others, it is equally important that we provide our own support. It will be vital for you to allow yourself to be alone and to rely on yourself at this time. You may feel panicky at first, but eventually you will be able to be alone and actually feel good about it. Start by trying to spend five minutes alone without music, television, or any other distraction. Unplug the telephone, and ask your children to play outside. Sit quietly, breathe deeply, and allow your feelings to come up. You can handle whatever pain comes up. You can handle being alone.

Allow yourself to mourn the loss of your parent completely. Get a stuffed animal and hold it tightly to comfort your inner child, for it is she who will be hurting the most. Love and comfort yourself. Spend time in bed, curled up in the fetal position, and let yourself howl and cry. Even though you may be tempted to run away from your pain, anger, loneliness, despair, and neediness, experiencing all of these feelings will actually help to dissipate your pain. Honor your needs and your feelings. Show concern for yourself by taking long, hot baths or by napping each afternoon. As surely as if you were recovering from a long illness or from surgery, you need to be careful with yourself and not expect too much from yourself. Take it easy, and take it slowly.

Mourn all your losses. Mourn all the things you missed out on as a child and adolescent. Mourn the loss of your full potential, the loss of "normalcy." Mourn the loss of hope. Feel the sadness of letting go.

It will also be important to realize that everyone reacts to pain differently. Don't be critical or judgmental of yourself if you begin to react in extreme ways or ways that are not typical of you. During your time of grieving, you may need to be more active or more quiet than usual. You may need to talk more or be alone to contemplate and feel more. You may need to express feelings out loud, or you may prefer to write them down in a journal. You may tend to rely on work, responsibility, or creativity to bolster your self-esteem, or you may need time away from responsibility. Taking care of yourself may mean keeping your hands busy or being physically active. Reading inspirational books, poetry, or autobiographies of courageous survivors may provide you with needed encouragement.

## UNRESOLVED GRIEF

Healthy grieving is a three-stage process of fully experiencing and expressing all of our emotions and reactions to our loss, letting go of our attachment to our parent and our sorrow, and, finally, recovering and reinvesting anew in our own life. Skipping any of these steps may result in unhealthy or unresolved grief.

The most extreme form of unresolved grief is absent grief, in which we become numb and have no reaction at all. This suppression of our natural grief can cause some rather severe problems. For example, it can cause our emotions to become deadened or distorted, our relationships to suffer, and our functioning to be impaired. As I stated earlier, even those whose parents were severely abusive and rarely caring suffer feelings of loss when they divorce their parents. If you find that you feel no grief whatsoever after several months of having no contact with your parent, you may be blocking your feelings.

We are denying our grief when we pretend not to feel. Fear of our feelings or of their intensity, fear of losing control, embarrassment about crying, and a need to put on a false front are all things that inhibit grief.

Often, we are afraid to confront grief feelings when they are at their strongest, and we imagine that delaying grief will make it easier later on. We may also delay grieving in order to maintain our functioning. Clients frequently tell me, "I'm afraid to get into my grief because I have this big assignment at work I just have to finish. If I start feeling my pain over the loss of my parent, I'll probably fall apart and not be able to work." Unfortunately, in delaying the grieving process we are bottling up pain that will erupt at some later time or in some other area of our lives, leaving us open to an unexpected emotional explosion.

Many factors can trigger the grief that was avoided earlier. These can be anything from a particular movie or book to an illness, the loss of a job, an accident, the birth of a child, a marriage, and, especially, holidays or other dates that hold significance for you. "Anniversary reactions," which are common for everyone, will be even more potent for you if your feelings about the loss have been suppressed.

It is far healthier for us to allow our feelings of loss to emerge when they present themselves, and to then release them, than to wait for a "convenient" time or for a time when we feel "ready." There is no better time than the present when it comes to allowing yourself to complete the grieving process. In so doing, you can finally let go of the past.

## COMPLETING THE GRIEVING PROCESS

Often, our grief is unfinished because we have found no comfortable means of releasing the complicated and mixed feelings we may have about our parent. The following exercise is an extremely effective tool for uncovering your hidden feelings and completing your grief process. Some people are able to complete their grief work during one session, while others work their way toward completion more slowly.

Find a quiet place to do this exercise, somewhere where you will not be disturbed. Plan to spend at least 30 to 45 minutes doing the exercise, and allow yourself the necessary time and space afterward to quietly stay with your feelings.

1. Sit in a chair with an empty chair facing you. Sit quietly for a few minutes and breathe deeply.

2. Imagine that your divorced parent is sitting in the chair facing you. You may want to place a picture of your parent on the chair, or an object that reminds you of him or her.

3. Speaking out loud, tell your parent whatever comes to mind that feels unfinished for you. Try to start your sentences with "I." For example, you might start with "I am still having trouble saying good-bye to you" or "I don't seem to have any feelings about not having you in my life."

4. After you say your opening sentence, your feelings may come rushing out. Say whatever you feel out loud.

5. If you feel stuck and don't have any feelings coming forth, try saying either "I am still angry with you" or "I still miss you." These statements should elicit some feelings. If you find that a particular statement does elicit strong feelings, or if you suspect that you have more feelings in a certain area, keep repeating that sentence until the feelings begin to surface. Allow yourself to feel whatever emotions emerge, and continue expressing these emotions out loud in "I" statements.

6. Another expression that may help evoke hidden feelings is "I wish . . . " Often, our secret wishes keep us from letting go and fully acknowledging our losses. Or you might say, "I know that I am not going to see you again." Pay attention to how you feel, and continue to express your feelings out loud.

7. Continue until you have nothing more to say. To test whether there is more that you need to express, state, "I feel finished with you now." See if this feels like the truth. If it doesn't, or if you are unsure, say, "I don't feel finished with you yet."

8. To complete the exercise and to test whether you are ready to say your final good-bye, say out loud, "I am ready to say good-bye to you now," and then also say, "I am not ready to say good-bye to you yet." See which one feels like the truth. If you feel ready, say your final good-bye, expressing any feelings that emerge.

9. You may wish to extend this exercise by also playing the role of your divorced parent, as you did when you practiced confrontations. This can give you the opportunity for real insight and objectivity, and it may help you to complete your grieving in an even more effective way.

Sit in the other chair, facing the seat where you have been sitting until now. Allow yourself to speak for your parent in response to the things you have said. If it feels right, you can have a dialogue between you and your parent, changing chairs as you do so.

All the intense feelings of mourning do gradually diminish and disappear, even though at times it may feel as though the pain is going to be endless. Letting go of your parent will be one of the hardest things you will ever have to do in your life, but it will also be one of the most rewarding things you can ever do for yourself. As you recover from grief, you will develop new strengths. Very often, facing a loss in our lives forces us to reeavaluate ourselves and results in a surge of personal growth and achievement.

CHAPTER 8

# New Beginnings and Happy Endings

Happy endings come in all forms. Divorcing a parent can be a very positive thing, bringing new changes and new growth. It can be the most productive, loving thing you have ever done for yourself. This does not mean that it won't occasionally be difficult for you to weather the storms of life without your parent or, in some cases, your entire family. And it doesn't mean that it won't be painful for you to celebrate the holidays without them. But overall, the pluses *far* outweigh the minuses for those whose relationships with their parents have become intolerable.

New beginnings can take various forms. Divorcing a parent will undoubtedly cause you to change in some way. You may change your behavior, your values, your attitudes, or your way of living. You may suddenly be motivated to take a totally new course of action, or you may commit yourself more intensely to the course of action you have already chosen. It can be a turning point in your life or a step along your way to recovery.

## NEW BEGINNINGS

Just as sometimes happens when a parent dies, some people experience a life transition after divorcing a parent. Michelle, for example, told me,

There was a part of me that felt so relieved after the divorce. I experienced a newfound freedom. It was like a new beginning. Permeating this, however, was the realization that now I had to grow up—I didn't have my mother to blame for all my problems anymore. This caused me to look at myself in an entirely different way. I started taking more responsibility for my own actions instead of constantly blaming others. I started looking at the way I have treated others in my life, and I was dismayed to realize how much I have hurt other people. I began to see how very much like my mother I turned out to be, even though it was the last thing I'd ever wanted to have happen. This caused me to begin to make some significant changes in my personality. Although it's taken time, I have made many of those changes, and I'm a much better person today because of them.

Zev also made some significant changes after divorcing his parents:

Divorcing my parents caused me to hit bottom. They were all the family I had, so it felt like I had to start all over to create a new family for myself. Before the divorce, I was far too dependent on my family for everything—feedback, money, a sense of self. Now I rely on myself more and have created a whole new support system of caring, loving people.

Megan made a life-changing transformation when she divorced her mother:

Divorcing my mother was the best thing I ever did for myself. It gave me a whole new life—one that wasn't dictated by criticism, judgments, and someone else telling me what to do. It gave me the opportunity to find out what I could do once I got out from under her tyranny. Now when I think of my life I see it in two distinct parts, which I call "B.D." and "A.D."—for before the divorce, and after the divorce. That's how different my life is now.

Marjorie discovered that by divorcing her parents she was able to break away from, and *stay* away from, other abusive people as well.

One of the main benefits of divorcing my parents is that if I hadn't done so I would have always had a person in my life that I was dependent upon. When I made the statement to my parents that I wouldn't be treated like this, that I refused to be treated badly by them, it made it a lot easier to say this to others who were abusive to me.

My parents' goal was to keep me incapacitated. They were invested in making me feel ineffectual. I knew I could always rely on my father to do the maintenance on my car, to fix things when they were broken, to make my decisions for me. After I divorced my parents, I discovered that I could make it financially without them and that I could handle my own life responsibly.

I discovered that these bargains that you make with your parents aren't really bargains at all. It may seem like a good idea to always know that you'll be taken care of by your parents, but it's not worth it. The whole premise is that you're not able to take care of yourself. Now I feel a tremendous satisfaction in realizing that I am *not* incompetent. I can do it myself, whatever it is. Letting go of my parents taught me that there isn't going to be anyone else to bail me out. I had to let go of my fantasy that someone was always going to rescue me.

Surviving a divorce can give you the courage and strength to tackle other problem areas of your life, as Patricia was able to do:

After I divorced my father I realized that I now had the courage to also divorce my husband, who was, in fact, very much like my father. I had been unhappy for a long time in the marriage but had hung on, just as I had with my father, hoping against hope that someday he would change and would appreciate me. In the process of readying myself for divorcing my father, I guess I was unconsciously doing the same with my husband. It was surprising how easy it actually was to divorce a husband who had been neglectful and cold once I realized he would never change and that I deserved much, much more.

Some adult children find that the divorce from their parent actually strengthens their marriage. This is exactly what happened to Fran:

Robert was so incredibly supportive of me throughout it all. I was really surprised, because I had never experienced him that way. But he knew what I had been through with my parents, and he believed I was doing the right thing. He helped see me through the ordeal of having to mourn both of my parents at the same time. He held me and encouraged me to cry, never making me feel bad for "carrying on," as my parents had always done when I was hurting. I felt completely accepted and loved by him, and it felt wonderful. We're closer than ever now.

The opposite can also be true. In some cases, the divorce of a parent can lead to the breakup of a relationship, as it did in Frank's case:

I realized that Mia couldn't be depended on in times of need. Here I was, devastated at my loss, and she just kept saying that I would get over it soon. She became bored with me because I "wasn't any fun anymore." She didn't seem to understand what I was going through, and she didn't seem to *want* to understand it. She just wanted me to get over it so we could go out and do things again. I'm glad I saw this side of her when I did, not after getting married.

New beginnings can also occur in your career when you divorce a parent. Nine months after divorcing her father, Celeste was able to quit a job that had been making her very unhappy. For 10 years she had endured a boss who was as critical, domineering, and controlling as her father.

It didn't even dawn on me that I didn't deserve this kind of treatment. I was so used to being criticized by my father that I put up with the same kind of treatment from my boss. It wasn't until I'd had the courage to divorce my father and had experienced what life was like without his constant berating that I became strong enough to quit my job.

## HAPPY ENDINGS

Deep inside, most adult children who have divorced their parents have a secret dream of getting back together and working things out. Even though they knew at the time that divorce was the

healthiest choice they could make, after some time apart many
adult children know they still love their parent and long for a
reconciliation. Peter's story had a happy ending:

> I felt very good about the fact that I was able to divorce my father. I
> didn't do it to punish him or to manipulate him, but to make a
> strong statement to him that I could not tolerate his current be-
> havior. I didn't speak to him for over three years. A lot happened to
> me in those three years. Because I wasn't around his abusiveness
> and because of therapy, my self-esteem improved greatly. I married
> a wonderful woman, and we have two children. I am a very success-
> ful photographer with my own business.
>
> I felt good about myself and my life, and I wanted to share some
> of it with my dad, if he wasn't still abusive. I wanted him to meet
> my wife and kids, and I guess there was also a part of me that
> wanted him to see that I was successful and had turned out well,
> not because of him but in spite of him.
>
> We've been in touch again for some time. I can't tell you it's all
> been a bed of roses, because it hasn't. From time to time his abusive
> nature rears its ugly head. But I am so strong now that I just don't
> allow it. When he starts to put me down or starts to tell me what to
> do, I just disengage from him for a while, and he gets the message.
> I guess those three years apart had a stronger impact on him than I
> ever imagined they would.

Like Peter, some adult children discover that being away from
their parent has made them much healthier and stronger—so
much so that they find they can now take much better care of
themselves when they are with their parent. Tanya gave her relationship with her parents one more try:

> I am no longer a child around my parents. It took not being around
> them for four years before I could say that, but I'm finally able to
> hold my own with them. I no longer feel afraid of them, of what
> they might say or do to hurt me. I no longer feel like their victim
> but like their equal. I can stand toe to toe with them and stand up
> for my rights. I know I couldn't have done it before because I was
> just too dependent on them. I had to prove to myself that I could
> make it without them. Now, I can even make it *with* them.

As time passes and as old wounds heal, it is natural to feel
more forgiving of even the cruelest parents and to miss even the

most unlovable ones. Harriet, who hadn't seen or heard from either of her parents in over eight years, certainly found this to be true.

Even though I don't regret divorcing them, I found that the more time went by, the more I was able to forgive them for the way they had treated me. And as more time passed, I also found that I missed them in my life. I decided to see them one more time to determine whether they had changed at all and whether we could get along any better. I realized that since so much time had passed I had probably forgotten how cruel they could be and how terrible I felt around them, and that there was a risk that out of missing them I had probably emphasized their positive qualities in my mind. But I had to find out. I saw my reconciliation attempt as giving me a chance to see the truth—whatever it might be.

I was pleasantly surprised by their response when I called. My mother sounded elated and called out to my father, "Harriet's on the phone! Harriet's on the phone!" Much to my surprise, he got on the phone immediately and said hello. There was no hesitation in his voice, and none of the old bitterness. We agreed to get together the next Sunday.

I was very nervous as I got ready to go see them. The long car drive gave me plenty of time to review in my mind my life with them and the years of being apart. I hadn't forgotten their cruelty, but I realized that I wasn't as afraid of them now. I felt more confident that I could defend myself against any potential cruelty I might encounter from them.

When my mother opened the door, she looked so happy to see me it made me cry. We hugged each other immediately, and it felt so good to feel her warmth. I noticed my dad in the background, looking uncomfortable and rather shy, very unlike what I had anticipated he'd be like. I remembered him as an imposing figure, always angry and gruff. Eight years had aged him tremendously. He didn't look threatening now at all. I approached him and stuck out my hand. He looked very nervous, but he tentatively took my hand for just a second or two. I looked him straight in the eye, and I noticed that he couldn't look at me the same way. He looked ashamed. But I caught his eye for just a moment. For just that one moment, our eyes locked and we made contact. It felt good. I realized that he had not looked me in the eye since he first began sexually molesting me. I had forgiven him for betraying me, and now with just that one look it seemed that he knew it.

While the three of us talked that afternoon, I realized that in the years that we'd been apart I had grown up. I was no longer afraid of them. I talked to them as their equal, not as a frightened little child. It also became evident that they had had plenty of time to realize just how much they had damaged me. My mother cried often, telling me how much she had missed me and how she regretted so many things, most especially the fact that she had not believed me when I told her my father had molested me. But she also told me that she had finally been able to confront him about my accusation, and that he had admitted to her that he had, indeed, abused me. I looked over at him. He nodded his head and said, "Yes, I told her the truth. I did molest you, and I am sorry. I'm sorry I didn't admit it much earlier."

It is not necessary for you to forgive your parents in order to reconcile with them. You may not be ready or able to forgive by the time you are ready to attempt a reconciliation. Perhaps during the reconciliation process itself, you may obtain enough trust and healing to be able to forgive. Or, you may never be able to forgive them.

"You might be asking, "How can this be? If I don't forgive, how can I possibly reconcile?" There are several ways this can happen. First of all, if you can really accept the fact that everyone is both good *and* bad, it is possible to love others for their good qualities in spite of what they have done to hurt you. Some people find that they can forgive the person, even though they cannot forgive the act.

You are the only one who can decide about forgiveness or reconciliation in your own case. You are the only one who will know whether the time is right. Trust your instincts, follow your heart, and do not allow circumstances or people to pressure you into a decision prematurely.

Even if they don't believe there can be a complete reconciliation, many adult children want to see the divorced parent again before he dies. Philip, who is gay, recounted the following to his support group after he had been to see his father:

Our meeting was very strained, and it was obvious that we were still very uncomfortable with each other. But I could see that he had missed me, and I realized I had missed him, too. I am sure he has never fully accepted my lifestyle, but he did have the courtesy to ask me about my life, how things were going. And he seemed genuinely interested—it wasn't fake. I feel good that I went to see him, because it turned out to be our last time together before he died. It felt good to know that some of the hurt and animosity between us had subsided. I felt more able to go on with my life, with fewer regrets and a stronger sense of pride.

Before attempting a reconciliation, ask yourself the following questions:

1. Are you being pressured into the reconciliation (for example, by illness, family wishes, religious beliefs, or guilt)?

2. Do you feel strong enough to defend yourself and to maintain your own separate identity?

3. Has your parent shown some signs of being willing to change? Is she willing to go into therapy with you or separately? Is she willing to work out a new relationship?

4. Has enough time elapsed to enable both of you to look at the reasons for the divorce, to see how each of you has changed, and to recognize how you really feel about each other now?

5. Is your parent ready to reconcile with you? Or is he still angry with you for blaming him, for being angry with him, for not having seen him for a while, or for divorcing him? He may need more time to heal and to forgive, no matter how forgiving *you* might feel.

If you decide to attempt a reconciliation, make sure that you can take care of yourself both emotionally and physically, and that you will be able to retain your sense of self when you are with your parent. It is also important to realize that the only way a reconciliation can work is if both parties have undergone some significant change. If this has not been the case, old patterns of behaving and coping are bound to reappear. The following suggestions can help you to make the most of your reconciliation efforts:

> *Be realistic; do not expect it to be easy.* Have reasonable expectations of the relationship instead of expecting everything to be different and wonderful. Otherwise, you will be disappointed and may give up before you have really started.
>
> *Make sure you have a plan of action.* Do not expect things to just "work out" without effort on both your parts. If you have no plan, you will find that you will fall back into old behavior patterns and negative ways of communicating.

- [ ] Set aside regular time for family meetings, a time to hash out some of the problems instead of letting them build up.

- [ ] Actively work on learning to communicate effectively with one another. Ask your parent to go into therapy with you to work out some of the problems and to improve communication. Read books on effective communication skills.

> *Make a mutual agreement.* As with all reconciliations, it is necessary for you and your parent to make a mutual agreement to bury the hatchet and go on. This means that you must call a cease-fire and work together toward establishing a peace treaty. Your agreement might include the following joint commitments:

- [ ] We will not continue to fight and be verbally abusive to each other. We will talk things out, look for solutions, and seek outside help when needed.

- [ ] We agree to listen to one another. (This may mean that you must take turns talking while the other listens, making no comments.)

- [ ] We agree to stop blaming each other. It is okay to express anger, but we will confine our statements to "I" statements, such as "I feel angry with you, because it sounds as though you don't completely believe what I am telling you," instead of "You still don't believe me—you're calling me a liar."

☐ We will try to explain why we are angry instead of just flying off the handle.

You may not be ready for a cease-fire if your anger is still so intense that all you want to do is rage at your parent. The same is true for your parent. If either or both of you cannot get past the anger long enough to make some agreements, then the time is not right for reconciliation. Perhaps more time needs to be spent apart, with each of you releasing your anger in constructive ways or working on your problems in therapy.

If you and your parent decide to begin seeing each other again, make sure you take it slow and easy. You've been out of each other's life for a while now, and it's likely that you've both changed in the process. Your parent hasn't been the center of your world, and you haven't been the center of his. You have new people in your life, new interests, and so on. Following are some suggestions on how to ease back into each other's lives:

See each other less often than you used to.

See each other for shorter periods of time.

If you are still somewhat afraid of your parent, try seeing him only when there are others present.

Work at communicating your needs better, such as saying no when you do not want to do something.

Work hard at not slipping into the old patterns of letting your parent control you or of trying to change your parent.

Even with all the positive changes that can come with divorcing a parent, many adult children don't consider the process complete unless they are able to successfully reconcile. Some who try are pleased with the results, finding that since they have become stronger and more mature they are now able to have a relationship with their parents that is far healthier than ever before.

On the other hand, some attempts at reconciliation simply reinforce the adult child's resolve to remain estranged from the parent. It is sometimes necessary to try a reconciliation in order to quiet the incessant doubting and internal questioning. Attempts that do not work out should never be seen as failures. After all, you can control only your end of any relationship. Although you may want a reconciliation with all your heart, your parent may not be willing or able to reciprocate. It is self-defeating to carry around a deep longing for the day when your relationship with your parent will magically transform, if all evidence points to the contrary. Saying your final good-bye can be the ultimate in happy endings. As wise philosophers have said, we must discard the old, unneeded baggage of our lives to make room for the new. By leaving a void in our lives, we are providing space for good things to enter.

Divorcing a parent is not about hate. It is about love. It is about loving yourself enough to give yourself the gift of freedom— freedom from the tyranny or deprivation of your childhood, freedom from the guilt and shame of never having felt that you were enough. It is giving yourself the freedom to become yourself and to accept yourself just the way you are. Divorcing a parent is about loving your parent—loving her even though you must love yourself more, and even though you have to let go. It is feeling the pain of losing someone you love, but all the while loving yourself for your strength, courage, and determination, and for your will to live a happy and productive life in spite of all your obstacles.

# To the Divorced Parent

If your adult child has divorced you or temporarily separated from you, and you find that as much as you miss him, as much as you want to reconcile with him, you stubbornly refuse to reach out to him, you may be doing what is called "distancing." Distancing can be either a conscious or unconscious defense against pain. It works like this: someone hurts your feelings, and you feel humiliated, devastated, all bad. Because you reacted so extremely, and because you feel so hurt and humiliated, the person who hurt you becomes associated with pain. Some of us are less willing than others to experience our pain. Some have such an aversion to pain that they want to avoid it at all costs, including entirely eliminating from their lives those who have hurt them. Distancing can cause us to write people off, to be in the same room and act as if they are not there, to convince ourselves that we no longer care when we still do.

In order to get your daughter or son back, you will need to swallow your pride, for it is probably your pride that in the past has prevented you from listening and admitting when you have been wrong.

You may want to read Part I of this book, which can help you to gain some insight into why your child has taken this drastic measure. On the other hand, you probably aren't totally in the dark as to her reasons for this estrangement. Chances are that you have been aware of the fact that she has been unhappy with you or the relationship for quite some time.

She may have been distant and withdrawn from you for a long time but you may have neglected to ask her what was wrong. She may have tried to tell you about how you have hurt her or about behavior or attitudes of yours that offend her, but you may not have been willing to listen. If you would like to reestablish the relationship with your child, you will need to be willing to listen to her now. And if you feel you have already listened, you will need to do so in a different way than you have done before. Perhaps you need to just listen and not talk back—not defend yourself, not argue, not correct what you think are inaccuracies. Just listen.

It is difficult to sit quietly and listen as someone tells you about all of the bad things you have done, reminds you of your shortcomings, or blames you for his unhappiness and problems. But if you want your child back in your life, this is exactly what you must be willing to do. You must listen with an open mind, with an eagerness to learn the truth.

Your child may tell you it is too late, that he has already tried to talk to you, but to no avail. Whatever the specific issue or issues involved, the bottom line usually comes down to this: most adult children want their parent to admit what he or she has done to hurt and damage them, and to apologize to them.

In order to do this, you must be willing to take a good hard look at yourself. When you look back at how you raised your child and on the ways that you have treated him, both as a child and as an adult, do you have any regrets? Can you think of things you may have done or left undone that might have hurt or damaged your child? Chances are that many of the things you think of may be some of the things your adult child remembers and still feels hurt about. The poem "Children Learn What They Live" may help you to understand what it is your child needed from you but did not get.

## CHILDREN LEARN WHAT THEY LIVE

Author Unknown

If a child lives with criticism, he learns to condemn

If a child lives with hostility, he learns how to fight

If a child lives with ridicule, he learns to be shy

If a child lives with shame he learns to feel guilty

If a child lives with tolerance, he learns to be patient

If a child lives with encouragement, he learns confidence

If a child lives with praise, he learns to appreciate

If a child lives with fairness, he learns justice

If a child lives with security, he learns to have faith

If a child lives with approval, he learns to like himself

If a child lives with acceptance and friendship, he learns to find love in the world

If you still feel stuck in terms of understanding why your child has divorced you, perhaps it will help you to review your own past and think about how *you* were treated as a child. If you were abused physically, verbally, or sexually, or neglected, overly controlled, or criticized, chances are very high that you abused your own children in the same ways. Research shows that those who were abused as children are far more likely to become abusive parents than those who were not abused. There are four basic categories of child abuse:

1. Physical abuse, corporal punishment or willful physical cruelty

2. Physical neglect, inadequate supervision, abandonment

3. Emotional abuse and deprivation

4. Sexual molestation, abuse, and sexual exploitation

PHYSICAL ABUSE.

Physical abuse refers to any nonaccidental injury, including violent assault with an implement such as a belt, strap, switch, cord, brush, or paddle, resulting in bruises, welts, burns, broken bones, fractures, scars, or internal injuries. "Spanking" for purely disciplinary reasons is not generally regarded as child abuse, although if bruises result or if a tool is used, it may be judged to be child abuse. Physical abuse includes being punched, slapped, pulled or yanked, choked, shaken, kicked, pinched, or tortured with tickling. It also includes the witnessing of violence done to a parent or sibling.

### PHYSICAL NEGLECT.

This includes abandonment; refusal to seek, allow, or provide treatment for illness or impairment; inadequate physical supervision; disregard of health hazards in the home; failure to provide adequate nutrition, clothing, or hygiene when services are available; keeping a child home from school repeatedly without cause; or failing to enroll a child in school.

### EMOTIONAL ABUSE.

Such abuse includes emotional or verbal assaults, including persistent teasing, belittling, or verbal attacks; close confinement, such as tying a child up or locking him in a closet, inadequate nurturing, such as that affecting failure-to-thrive babies; putting unreasonable demands on a child; knowingly permitting antisocial behavior, such as delinquency; or ignoring a diagnosed emotional problem.

### SEXUAL ABUSE.

Sexual abuse covers sexual molestation; incest; exploitation for prostitution; the production of pornographic materials; or any other exploitation of a child for the sexual gratification of an adult. This can include physical sexual abuse, indirect sexual abuse, verbal sexual abuse, boundary violation, and emotional sexual abuse.

> *Physical sexual abuse* includes sexualized hugging or kissing, sexual fondling, oral or anal sex, intercourse,

masturbation of the victim, or forcing of the victim to masturbate the offender.

*Indirect sexual abuse* includes any act of voyeurism or exhibitionism on the part of an adult toward a child for the conscious or unconscious sexual stimulation of the adult. With voyeurism, the adult becomes sexually stimulated by watching a child dress, undress, take a bath or shower, or use the toilet. Exhibitionism is when the adult exposes his genitals to the child or walks around naked for the purpose of being sexually stimulated.

*Verbal sexual abuse* includes using inappropriate sexual words or obscenities in an abusive way toward a child, asking inappropriate questions about the child's sexual life or sexual anatomy, talking about sex in front of a child whose age level is inappropriate, or making remarks about the sexual parts of the child's body (for example, remarks about the size of the child's breasts or penis).

*Boundary violation* includes exposure of children to their parents' sexual behavior or naked bodies. It also includes the denying of privacy to a child such as walking in on the child in the bathroom or in his or her bedroom.

*Emotional sexual abuse* occurs when one or both parents bond inappropriately with one of the children. When a parent uses a child to meet his or her emotional needs, the relationship can easily become sexualized and romanticized. Pia Mellody, an expert on codependence, defines emotional sexual abuse as occurring "when one parent has a relationship with the child that is more important than the relationship [that parent has] with [the] spouse."

Ask yourself whether you were abused in any of the above ways when you were a child, and whether you have in turn abused your child in any of these ways. It is not your fault that you were abused, but you are responsible for your own actions as an adult as a consequence of that abuse. You will need to acknowledge to your child that your behavior was abusive, apologize, and ask her what she needs from you now. She may need only an apology for your having abused her in the past. An honest apology from an abusive or neglectful parent can be incredibly healing to an adult child. Or, it may be that you are still being abusive in some way and need to begin working on your problems, whatever they may be. You may need to join groups such as Parents United (for sexually abusive parents and their partners), Parents Anonymous (for parents who have been physically abusive to their children), Alcoholics Anonymous (for alcoholics or alcohol abusers), Al-Anon (for partners and relatives of alcoholics), or CODA (for codependents)—whatever applies to you. You may also need to seek therapy. It would also be a positive gesture for you to offer to pay for your child's therapy if she tells you that she has required treatment because of your abusive behavior toward her.

Even if you are able to listen to your child, admit the mistakes you have made, and apologize for your actions, don't expect your adult child to be willing to reconcile right away. He will probably still have a tremendous amount of anger that he will need to release first. Much of this anger can be released in therapy or in ways that don't involve you. However, your child may need to release his anger directly toward you in order to heal from the abuse. As the ultimate act of love and kindness, you might consider allowing your child to vent his anger toward you in person. As Alice Miller writes in her book *For Your Own Good,*

> The greatest cruelty that can be inflicted on children is to refuse to let them express their anger and suffering except at the risk of losing their parents' love and affection. The anger stemming from early childhood is stored up in the unconscious, and since it basically represents a healthy, vital source of energy, an equal amount of energy must be expended in order to repress it.

Above all, your adult child deserves to have you treat her with respect. This may mean not getting drunk in front of her, not making derogatory remarks to her, or not looking at her seductively. It may mean treating her as an adult instead of a child, and not trying to control her or tell her how to run her life. Above all, it means letting go and letting your child *be*—or, in the words of Kahlil Gibran in *The Prophet,*

> " . . . Your children are not your children.
> They are the sons and daughters of Life's longing for itself.
> They come through you but not from you,
> And though they are with you yet they belong not to you.
>
> You may give them your love but not your thoughts,
> For they have their own thoughts.
> You may house their bodies but not their souls,
> For their souls dwell in the house of tomorrow, which you cannot
>     visit, not even in your dreams,
> You may strive to be like them, but seek not to make them like you.
> For life goes not backward nor tarries with yesterday . . . "

# To Mates, Friends, and Other Loved Ones

It is difficult to understand why someone would want to go to the extreme of divorcing a parent unless you yourself have had to resort to such an extreme. If your parents were not abusive, neglectful, controlling, or critical, you probably have a difficult time relating to a mate or friend who has been severely damaged by a parent. It's always difficult to empathize with someone whose experience has been totally different from ours. Instead, we may want to convince our loved one that it couldn't have been so bad. We try to apply logic: "After all, if your parent had really been that horrible to you, you wouldn't have turned out so well." Or, we may try to offer hope and advice: "Maybe if you just try a little harder . . ." In reality, however, we are just offering false hope and putting the blame and burden back on the shoulders of the abused person.

It hurts us to realize that someone we love could have been hurt so much. And it hurts us to know that our loved one will have to suffer even further from the loneliness and pain of not seeing a parent. We want to take the pain away somehow. We can't believe that divorcing the parent is the only alternative—surely, we think, there must be something else that can be done.

Divorcing a parent certainly is a radical extreme, and you may have never heard of it as a healthy option for adult children. But as radical as it may seem, it has been proved to be a healthy choice for those whose parents were or still are physically, verbally, or sexually abusive; overly controlling; or hypercritical. By reading this book, you will have gained a better understanding of the reasons why some adult children choose to divorce a parent. In addition, the following suggestions will help you to be better able to support your loved one.

Often, our own issues get in the way of our being able to fully support someone who chooses to divorce a parent. Because of these issues, we cannot be objective. Here are some of the things that might be in your way of being able to be supportive toward your friend or loved one:

DENIAL.

This denial may be about your own childhood, about any abuse that you or someone else in your family has suffered, or about the reality that such terrible things do happen to people.

Those who have the hardest time understanding another person's need to divorce a parent seem to be those who have suffered abusive childhoods themselves. Those who were raised by abusive, alcoholic, or hypercritical and overcontrolling parents are often in denial about how much they suffered as children and how much they continue to suffer from their parents' behavior and attitudes. Because of this denial, they become critical of those who are facing the truth about their own childhoods and parents. They may accuse these people of being vindictive, of holding on to the past, or of making a big deal out of nothing.

If you are extremely critical of your loved one's decision to divorce a parent, take a good look at the reasons for your attitude. If you haven't faced your own anger and pain concerning your childhood, you may have an investment in your loved one's not facing his or hers. It may make you feel very uncomfortable to be around someone who is facing feelings similar to ones that you buried long ago, since it may stir up memories and feelings that you would prefer to keep buried. Your denial may be hurting not only you, but your loved one as well.

FEAR.

You may have a fear of being judged by your own children as an unfit parent. You may have a fear of your own parents, of your own feelings of anger, and of what would happen to you if you divorced your parents. Or, you may have a fear of being divorced by your mate.

It seems that once we become parents ourselves we tend to want to forgive our parents for their shortcomings. Sometimes this comes out of a true understanding of how hard it is to raise children, but often it comes out of the fear that we ourselves are not being good parents. We suddenly become afraid that our own children will someday judge us harshly and complain that we ruined their lives.

When your friend or loved one talks to you about divorcing her parent, make sure your fear that your own children may someday want to divorce you doesn't get in the way of your being objective with her. Chances are that you are *not* being abusive or neglectful to your children. And that is what we are talking about here: parents who were physically, emotionally, or sexually abusive to their children or who deprived their children of adequate food, shelter, and nurturing—*not* parents who sometimes got angry at their children or were sometimes too busy to listen to them.

You need to be aware of your own issues and acknowledge how these issues might interfere with your objectivity. You and your friend or mate both need to understand that your attempts to protect her by trying to talk her out of divorcing a parent may actually stem from your own need to protect yourself. In addition, you will need you to do the following:

☐ Believe your friend or loved one when he tells you about how his parent abused, deprived, controlled, and otherwise damaged him. Know that it is far more likely that he is minimizing and denying how bad it really was than it is that he is making it up or exaggerating. Even if what he tells you sounds too extreme, believe that it really happened.

☐ Just listen; do not give advice. Your advice may actually end up being counterproductive, since you are not a trained professional and since the advice may be coming from your own need to protect yourself. The only advice your loved one may need from you is that he seek professional help if he has not done so already. Let him know you are open to hearing whatever he is willing to share.

☐ Tell him that you trust he will do what is best for him and that you will support him in whatever decision he makes. He probably already has difficulty trusting his own decisions and perceptions, and he needs to have these validated, not questioned.

☐ Let him know he will not be alone, that you will be there for him when he needs you. Tell him that even though he has lost his parent, he will have you as part of his new "family."

☐ Stand up for him when other people criticize him. Care for your loved one by supporting him in front of others and by letting others know that you trust he is doing the right thing.

☐ Know that abusive parents can be deceivingly charming. Don't get caught up in their game of looking good in order to discredit their child. If your loved one's parents try to convince you or others that their child is crazy or vindictive, make it clear that you believe him and support him in his decision.

☐ In speaking with your loved one, don't defend his parents, sympathize with them, or try to get him to be more understanding of them. He needs your absolute loyalty. If you have been close to his parents, you may have a desire for your loved one to forgive them so that relations can go on as they always have. But this may not be possible. You will have to go along with your loved one's decision, even if it's not your preference. To continue to relate on friendly terms with someone who has abused your loved one is a form of betrayal.

# To Therapists

I believe that forgiveness is a spiritual issue, not a therapeutic one. For this reason, I don't believe it is the therapist's place to push forgiveness on a client, any more than it is to push one's own religious beliefs. I believe we must leave our own opinions about forgiveness out of our work, as assuredly as we attempt to leave our religious beliefs out of it.

If you believe that forgiveness should be the ultimate goal for adult children, you have a right to your belief; however, you do not have the right to impose that belief on your clients. Not all therapists believe as you do. In fact, a growing number of professionals who work with adults who were abused as children are finding that many of their clients cannot forgive, and that not forgiving does not interfere with recovery. In other words, they are finding that forgiveness is not essential for healing.

It is up to the client to decide what to do regarding his or her parents. Our role is to offer our clients options, help them to come to the right decision *for them*, and to support whatever decision they make. Adult children of alcoholics or abusive families essentially have three options: to separate from their parents temporarily, to divorce them, or to reconcile with them. All of these options are healthy choices.

Divorcing a parent can, indeed, be a very healthy choice for adult children whose parents have been or continue to be abusive, neglectful, or overly controlling. Divorcing a parent can help a client to

☐ individuate

☐ stop being a victim

☐ break the cycle of violence

Discuss with your client both the possible benefits and the possible negative consequences, of divorcing a parent. Make sure your client is fully prepared for any consequence.

Your own personal history can influence whether you believe that divorcing a parent is or is not a healthy option. If you had a relatively healthy childhood, you may have a difficult time empathizing with those who have suffered severe physical, sexual, verbal, or emotional abuse. Therefore, it may also be difficult for you to understand why someone would want to divorce a parent. On the other hand, if you came from an abusive or alcoholic household, you may be in denial about your own anger and desire to disconnect from your parent. Sometimes a strong belief in forgiveness can be a way of denying and avoiding our own anger.

It is equally important that you do not try to influence your client *to* divorce a parent. If you yourself are an adult child of an alcoholic or abusive parent it is important that you work through your anger at your parent so that it doesn't spill over and cause you to push your client into divorcing his or her parent. If you believe strongly in divorcing parents, be careful not to be critical or impatient with clients who choose to reconcile with their parents or continue trying in their relationships with them. Remember that only the client knows what is right for him or her. Even though it is difficult to stand by when you see a client being continually damaged by a parent, once you have offered the option of divorce you need to keep quiet and let the client do what he or she needs to do.

As you know, divorcing a parent is an incredibly difficult task to accomplish and takes a tremendous amount of courage and strength. Your client may not be ready, and may never be ready, to sever the ties with his parents. In this case it will be important for you to work with him on ways for him to take care of himself while he is around his parent, to release his anger toward his parent, to mourn his lost childhood, and to give up fantasies of his parent's ever being the "good" parent.

If you are conducting a therapy group (for example, for adult children of alcoholics, incest survivors, or codependents), there may be a great deal of group pressure for one member to divorce an abusive parent. Make sure you balance this out with permission for the client to be herself and to do what is right for her regardless of what others say. Otherwise, she may either feel pressured into doing something she isn't ready to do or feel criticized for not divorcing her parent (and may thus drop out of the group).

Whether your client ultimately decides to reconcile with, temporarily separate from, or divorce an abusive parent, it is crucial that she release her anger. As her therapist, you need to teach her that anger is a natural and healthy response to the abuse and neglect she has suffered. Let her know that her anger is not something to be rushed through, and that if she chooses to forgive, she will be able to do this only after she has released her anger. Help her to release her anger so that she won't be divorcing her parent as a means of revenge or retaliation.

In order to work effectively with abuse victims, you will need to be comfortable with anger, rage, and violence. Clients who consider divorcing their parents have often been through devastating, violence-filled childhoods.

To help clients feel and express their anger, it is important that we as therapists work through our own anger. Otherwise, we will likely be afraid of our clients' anger and will give them the non-verbal message that we are threatened by their release of anger.

Believe your client when she tells you about her childhood, even if what she says happened may seem to you to be unbelievable—for example, acts of brutality, gross neglect, the sacrificing of children to other adults for sexual purposes, or sexual relations between both parents and the child. The atrocities are difficult to hear about and sometimes difficult to believe, but most adult clients do not lie or exaggerate about them. In fact, as experts in the field of child abuse understand, clients are more likely to minimize and deny the painful events of their childhoods—not the other way around. Clients may tell you horrible things, only to recant later on. This does not mean that they lied to you at first; most likely, they are simply experiencing another wave of denial.

It is also important that you encourage your client to speak out. This may include her confronting her parent directly or indirectly (for example, role-playing or writing letters she does not send), taking legal action, or disclosing the abuse to other family members. While you should never *push* a client into doing any of these things, if she chooses to speak out, support her. Be sure she is ready to handle the confrontation by helping her to prepare for it (perhaps through role-playing and "empty-chair" exercises). If possible, offer to facilitate confrontations or meetings between the client and her parent.

Above all, remember that you have a tremendous influence on adult children of dysfunctional families and therefore a tremendous responsibility. They will see you as a surrogate parent, a role model, and as a powerful authority figure. Even a subtle sign of disapproval from you regarding their desire to divorce a parent can make them throw out the idea entirely in an effort to please you or do the right thing. No matter what your personal beliefs are about forgiveness, or the sanctity of the family, you owe your clients to put your beliefs aside and to be as objective as humanly possible so that they will have the option of deciding for themselves whether they want to divorce a parent.

# References, Recommended Reading, and Resources

Bass, Ellen, and Laura Davis. *The Courage To Heal: A Guide for Women Survivors of Child Sexual Abuse.* New York: Harper & Row, 1988.

Bloomfield, Harold. *Making Peace With Your Parents.* New York: Ballantine, 1983.

—————. *Inner Joy: New Strategies for Adding Pleasure To Your Life.* New York: Jove Books, 1980.

Bradshaw, John. *The Family: A Revolutionary Way of Self-Discovery.* Deerfield Beach, Florida: Health Communications, 1988.

—————. *Healing The Shame That Binds You.* Deerfield Beach, Florida: Health Communications, 1988.

Black, Claudia. *It Will Never Happen To Me.* Denver, Colorado: M.A.C., 1982.

Davidson, Joy. *The Agony of it All: The Drive for Drama and Excitement in Women's Lives.* Los Angeles: Tarcher, 1988.

Dwinell, Lorie, and Jane Middleton-Moz. *After The Tears.* Pompano Beach, Florida: Health Communications, 1986.

Engel, Beverly. *The Right To Innocence: Healing The Trauma of Childhood Sexual Abuse.* Los Angeles: Tarcher, 1989.

Friday, Nancy. *My Mother My Self.* New York: Dell Publishing, 1977.

Forward, Susan. *Toxic Parents: Overcoming Their Hurtful Legacy and Reclaiming Your Life.* New York: Bantam, 1989.

Farmer, Steven. *Adult Children of Abusive Parents.* Los Angeles: Lowell House, 1989.

Gibran, Kahlil. *The Prophet.* New York: Alfred A. Knopf, 1986.

Gravitz, Herbert, and Julie Bowden. *Guide To Recovery: A Book for Adult Children of Alcoholics.* Holmes Beach, Florida: Learning Publications, Inc., 1985.

Halpern, Howard. *Cutting Loose: An Adult Guide To Coming To Terms With Your Parents.* New York: Bantam Books, 1976.

Miller, Alice. *The Drama of the Gifted Child: How Narcissistic Parents Form and Deform the Emotional Lives of Their Talented Children.* New York: Basic Books, 1981.

_____ . *For Your Own Good: Hidden Cruelty in Child-Rearing and The Roots of Violence.* New York: Farrar, Straus, Giroux, 1983.

_____ . *Thou Shalt Not Be Aware: Society's Betrayal of the Child.* New York: New American Library, 1986.

Pollard, John. *Self Parenting.* Malibu, Calif.: Generic Human Studies, 1987.

Norwood, Robin. *Women Who Love Too Much.* Los Angeles: Tarcher, 1985.

Talelbaum, Judy. *The Courage To Grieve.* New York: Harper & Row, 1980.

Viorst, Judith. *Necessary Losses.* New York: Fawcett, 1986.

Wegscgeuder-Cruse, Sharon. *Choice-Making: For Co-Dependents, Adult Children and Spirituality Seekers.* Pompano Beach, Florida: Health Communications, 1985.

Whitfield, Charles. *Healing the Child Within.* Pompano Beach, Florida: Health Communications, 1987.

Woititz, Janet. *Struggle For Intimacy.* Pompano Beach, Florida: Health Communications, 1985.

_____ . *Adult Children of Alcoholics.* Pompano Beach, Florida: Health Communications, 1983.

RESOURCES

## DIVORCING A PARENT WORKSHOPS
CASSA Counseling
205 Avenue I, Suite #27
Redondo Beach, CA 90277

# ABOUT THE AUTHOR

Beverly Engel, a licensed marriage, family, and child counselor, is an expert on the subject of child abuse and for seventeen years has been a therapist specializing in working with adult children of dysfunctional families. She is the founder and director of the Center of Adult Survivors of Sexual Abuse (CASSA) and has trained hundreds of professionals in how to work with survivors of dysfunctional families. Beverly Engel is the author of *The Right to Innocence: Healing the Trauma of Childhood Sexual Abuse* and maintains a private practice in Southern California.